Where Am 'I' *Right Now?*

Physically – Emotionally – Mentally – Spiritually

First Edition

2014

Adrian Hanks

Brisbane, Australia

Copyright © 2014 Adrian Hanks

All rights reserved. No part of the book may be transmitted or reproduced by any form or means, either mechanical or electronic, including recording and photocopying, or by any known storage and retrieval system, without the written consent of the author, except in the case of short quotations being used in a review.

National Library of Australia Cataloguing-in-Publication entry

Author:	Hanks, Adrian, author.
Title:	Where am 'I' right now? : physically – emotionally – mentally – spiritually / Adrian Hanks.
ISBN:	9780646924670 (paperback)
Subjects:	Self-actualization (Psychology)
	Conduct of life-Anecdotes.
	Spiritual life.
Dewey Number:	158.1

Publishers Details

Conscious Life Development Foundation

Brisbane, Australia

Contact Details: infoWAIRN@bigpond.com

The author of this book is not dispensing medical advice or prescribing the use of any technique as a form of treatment for medical, physical or emotional problems without the advice of a physician, either directly or indirectly.

His intent is to offer information only, to help you in your quest for spiritual and emotional well-being. In the event you use any of the information in this book for yourself, which is your divine right, the author and the publisher assume no responsibility for your actions.

For the Michael Age

We must eradicate from the soul all fear and terror

of what comes towards us out of the future.

We must acquire serenity in all feelings

and sensations about the future.

We must look forward with absolute equanimity

to everything that may come,

and we must think only that whatever comes,

is given to us by a world direction full of wisdom.

It is part of what we must learn in this age, namely,

to live out of pure trust without any security in existence,

trusting in ever present help of the spiritual world.

Truly, nothing else will do if our courage is not to fail us.

Let us discipline our will and let us seek

the awakening from within ourselves

every morning and every evening.

Rudolf Steiner, 1917

Contents

Acknowledgements ix

Welcome and Introduction xi

Preparation xiii

Chapter One
Starting the Where Am 'I' *Right Now?* Journey 1

Chapter Two
Understanding Ourselves from a Holistic and
Spiritual Perspective 12

Chapter Three
The Six Degrees of Conscious Development 31

Chapter Four
The Four Temperaments 48

Chapter Five
Ending the Blame Game 55

Chapter Six
Eco-Soul Bush Experience 60

Chapter Seven
Habits and Addictions 67

Chapter Eight
From Present Self to Future Potential Self 75

Chapter Nine
Creating Healthy Boundaries 79

Chapter Ten
Empowering Men 87

Chapter Eleven
Fear, Doubt and (Self) Hatred 93

Chapter Twelve
Thinking, Feeling and Willing 101

Chapter Thirteen
Reactions, Projections and Judgements 104

Chapter Fourteen
Dramatizing 110

Chapter Fifteen
Artistic and Creative Expression 120

Chapter Sixteen
Where Am 'I' *Right Now* with my Vocation or
Life Purpose 129

Chapter Seventeen
Where Am 'I' *Right Now* in my Family Life? 132

Chapter Eighteen
Where Am 'I' *Right Now* in my Social Life? 137

Chapter Nineteen
Where Am 'I' *Right Now* with my Intimacy? 140

Chapter Twenty
Where Am 'I' *Right Now* with my Sexuality? 144

Chapter Twenty One
Where Am 'I' *Right Now* in my Spiritual Life? 152

Chapter Twenty Two
Self-Care 162

Chapter Twenty Three
The Art of Communication 166

Chapter Twenty Four
The Three Word Homeopathic Poem 172

Chapter Twenty Five
Fun and Games 177

Chapter Twenty Six
The Destiny Basket..181

Chapter Twenty Seven
Meditation and Relaxation 186

Chapter Twenty Eight
Goal Setting 189

Chapter Twenty Nine
Procrastination 196

Chapter Thirty
Adrian's Story 199

Chapter Thirty One
The Botshabelo Community 217

Chapter Thirty Two
Rudolf Steiner 218

Further Information 221

Acknowledgements

To celebrate and honour the publication of this book, I would like to thank all the people who have helped me on my life journey thus far. There are many hundreds of people across the globe (and beyond) to thank, so Thank You!

Above all, I especially want to express my deepest love and gratitude to my beautiful best friend, colleague, mentor and loving wife, Arleen, who has offered and given her full encouragement, love and support since meeting me.

I would like to thank, with all my heart, my six wonderful children – yes six – Solomon, Alexander, Travis, Oliver, Genevieve and Timeah, my three delightful grandchildren, Alira, Misty and Alyssa for their beautiful grand-dad smiles and my two God-daughters Grace and Kala. Thanks also to my mother-in-law Eileen, for her patience, yummy food and supportive love.

Thanks and love goes to the rest of my family and friends that live far and wide for the love and support that they offer me. I want to heartily thank my mother for her gift of laughter and fun and my father for his love of nature and his quick mind, all of which I have fortunately inherited. To my brothers and sisters Alison, Ashley, James, Debbie and Sarah-Jane – love to you.

Thanks also to my good mate, Barry Auchettl, for being alongside me as a friend and Master-Mind partner whilst I was writing this book. Our regular weekly meetings over the past few years have been a solid rock for me.

Where Am 'I' Right Now?

To my many teachers (alive and passed on, human and non-human), you all deserve a big thank you. They include: my team of spirit guides, whom I have gathered over the years and Rudolf Steiner, Ian Gawler (Meditation), Peter Gingell (primary school teacher), Yehuda Tagar and Robin Steele (Psychophonetics), Jeff Levin (Life Alignment), Nelson Mandela, Eric Beach (poetry), Peter Malcolm (didgeridoo), the men from all the Men's Circles and of course my golfing buddies who share with me the greatest mind-game ever created!

No book is ever created without the support of a special team, so a big thank you to my special team. Robin Steele for ploughing through the big first editing job, Carlos for challenging me to 'homeopothise' my work, David and Chrissie and the team at Frontline Copy Centre in Byron Bay for all the printing and the many 'mock-ups', Tristan Caneris Photography for the front cover image, Ingram Sparks the printers and distributors, and finally a huge thanks to Julie-Ann and the team from the Pick-a-WooWoo Publishing Group for guiding me very sensitively and professionally through the publishing process.

Welcome and Introduction

Firstly, I want to wish you a very warm welcome and thank you sincerely for picking up this book. I am very excited for you, as I know that the contents of this book will positively change the way in which you live your life if you choose to read and work with the content being offered. I do not want to presume, judge or guess where you are *Right Now* in your life, physically, emotionally, mentally or spiritually, and regardless of where that place is, I trust that you will receive and gain something insightful, new and very positive.

There are many thousands of books available on personal and spiritual development and it is not always easy to know which ones to buy or read. Many of these books manage to direct and tell us 'what' to do in terms of being in the present moment or standing in our power, and even though we might receive a great deal of advice on reading about 'what' to do, many of these books often miss one of the most important ingredients – and that is – 'how' to do it – outlining and guiding us on 'how' we can develop, grow and be much more conscious and empowered in our lives.

This book is very much about 'how' we can all stand more consciously and fully in our power; standing in what I refer to throughout this book as, 'our 'I' presence', and no matter where you are *Right Now* in your life you will have a very real opportunity to build some new skills, knowledge, insights, wisdom, and understanding by engaging with what is offered to you in this book.

The essence and the driving force of my work is about supporting and encouraging, and when required, positively challenging people to explore, discover and engage with life in a more focused and conscious way – from one's centre – from one's 'I' presence. When working consciously from the position of our 'I' presence, I strongly believe that we can achieve just about anything that we wish to achieve in life – physically, emotionally, mentally and spiritually.

So get yourself comfortable and let us begin our journey with a little preparation …

Preparation

Before you delve into the book, I am going to ask you to do several things.

1. Go and find or buy a journal. Something with blank pages is good to use. You might like to have a highlighter to mark anything in this book which you feel is worth highlighting. I love to highlight and many of my books are full of colourful markings.

2. When you have a question, a deep thought, an intuitive feeling, or a moment of pure enlightenment that stems from reading this book, write it down in your journal.

3. Commit to trying to understand everything you read in this book, even if it means reading it two or even three times or doing a little research. This is where highlighting helps.

4. Complete all of the exercises and tasks in each chapter!

5. Have fun!

Chapter One

Starting the Where Am 'I' *Right Now?* Journey

Now that you are all prepared and organised with your new journal, it is time to move on and get you practically involved with the book.

> **Throughout this book you will be offered various exercises and tasks to work through. When you see the round Ying/Yang exercise image (see below), it is an indication for you to stop, take action and do the exercise or task.**

Each exercise will give you an opportunity to gather some new, powerful and effective personal tools to help you to further develop your skills for physical, emotional, mental and spiritual growth. Make it a personal challenge to complete each of the exercises before moving on to the next page or chapter. It is advisable to read through and understand each exercise before actually doing them, this way you will keep a better flow with the whole process.

Where Am 'I' Right Now?

As you may have realized from the name of the book, the main focus is about you asking yourself the question – **Where Am 'I' Right Now?**

This first exercise will help you to connect and begin your journey. Follow the exercise carefully and remember to use your *Right Now* journal as much as you can. I know from my own experience of journal work that by doing so you will be able to follow and gauge your journey and your results, which can be a very useful resource later on.

These next four questions could be the only questions you ever ask yourself on your journey of personal and professional development and that would be enough to keep you busy, alert and challenged every day for the rest of your life!

So, to begin with, answer (by writing in your journal) the following questions. There are no wrong answers. The answers you find within are the right ones for you. Just be as honest and authentic as you can and you will get much more out of it. You are not in competition with anyone, this is just about you.

Q 1: Where Am 'I' *Right Now* in my life – physically?

Q 2: Where Am 'I' *Right Now* in my life – emotionally?

Q 3: Where Am 'I' *Right Now* in my life – mentally?

Q 4: Where Am 'I' *Right Now* in my life – spiritually?

To give you some help and support with this first exercise I have outlined a few thoughts and ideas of what you might wish to address in each section.

Physically

By addressing the question of how you are physically, you might want to look at your physical fitness and exercise, your diet, your skin, your weight, your physical activities, your posture, your working conditions, your sleep patterns and even your physical sex life.

Emotionally

By exploring your emotional life you might like to look at your communication skills and how you are affected emotionally when communicating or interacting with people. You might also like to look at your feelings and emotions around your fears, doubts and sense of self-love. How do you feel about these things emotionally? Also, how are you emotionally when you are dealing with everyday situations like driving, working, studying, playing sport, socializing, being in relationship and being alone?

Mentally

How are you when using your mental faculties, like you are now reading this book and taking in new information? How sharp is your mind and how sharp is your thinking? How often do you have clear and precise thoughts without any confusion dimming your thoughts? How often do you exercise your mind with study or other mind processes?

Spiritually

Spirituality is an area in our lives where we can easily let things fade away or disappear completely if we are not following specific routines or exercises, such as meditation, prayer, ritual, study or inner reflection. Where are you in your own spiritual journey *Right Now*? What daily or weekly practice do you follow or tune into? How comfortable are you around spiritual topics and activities?

Take some time to ponder and explore these questions and then write each answer out in your journal. Each answer will give you a deeper sense of where you are *Right Now* and give you a great foundation from which to work from.

Try and bring these four questions into your daily life for a while. See if you can challenge yourself to ask them every day, on the hour, every hour, for at least one week. Yes – on the hour, every hour for one week. Of course this is for when you are awake during the day and not during your sleep time at night!

To fully engage in this exercise it is a good idea to actually set an alarm, either on your clock, watch or mobile phone to help you to do this more successfully. If doing this exercise every hour is too much for you, try doing it four times a day, although you will find that by doing it hourly each day it will increase your faculties of self-awareness much more rapidly.

This exercise or technique I call the 'Where Am 'I' *Right Now?* exercise' or the 'Where's *(add your name)* exercise'. It is a bit like the *Where's Wally* books, where we have to try and find Wally in amongst all the people!

By following this exercise you will find that you have the opportunity to check in with yourself to observe how you are doing physically, emotionally, mentally and spiritually and learn how to heighten your awareness and become more centred, focused and engaged in your daily life.

If you have a modality or a technique that you like to use, such as NLP or Gestalt, you can also use that to help you to lock this experience in. Please always feel free to use whatever tools you have at your disposal as an addition to what is on offer here in this book. The more tools you have in your personal development tool bag, the easier it will be to find the right tool when needed. The reality is, we generally like to use a combination of modalities, skills and experiences in our lives and I would like to encourage you to do that whilst reading this book. Creating our own unique and individual tool box is fun; filling it with tools which suit us best and with tools that we are most likely to use is the way to go.

If you can get into the habit of asking yourself the question – Where Am 'I' *Right Now*? on the hour, every hour or at least four times a day, every day and answer as authentically as you can in the four ways outlined: physically, emotionally, mentally and spiritually, it will totally change the way in which you live your life. This method is, paradoxically, simple yet very profound and even after just one week you will notice some big differences and will find that life is not quite the same as it ever was before.

Warning!

Doing this exercise will positively and dramatically change the way in which you live your life – Forever!

Carlos, a good friend of mine, who has participated in many Men's Circles over the years, did the Where Am 'I' *Right Now?* exercise for a few weeks after I introduced it to him in early 2010. He told me that it totally changed his life. He set his mobile phone alarm to go off every day, on the hour, every hour whilst at work and also at home in the evenings.

Where Am 'I' Right Now?

Here is what Carlos has to say about his experience.

Attending Adrian's Men's Group every week has always been an eye opening experience for me. It is very empowering to observe and learn from good men, and to then give birth to my own unique insights about who I really am, and who I really want to be. In my work life as a Real Estate agent, putting into practice my insights from Men's Group used to be a daunting and very difficult task. I was unhappily and stubbornly dedicating most of my entire existence to my role as a Property Manager. I had no real sense of my own needs, and very little sense of where I was heading in my life, other than to constant burn outs and nervous breakdowns from time to time. This was very sad and frustrating to say the least.

During a particular session of Men's Group, Adrian challenged all of us men to 'check in' on our power and centre ourselves throughout our day. The aim; to remain as aware as possible emotionally, mentally, physically and spiritually and to make the necessary adjustments to what is needed to remain in that centred state. In my experience, the world is a very difference place when I am centred and in full alignment. In this state, I catch glimpses of myself moving mountains and succeeding at the highest levels with ease. To stay centred is to stay true to myself and to others, and to truly step into living life from the sacred space of who I really am. This beauty was often squandered by the demands of busy life, and especially by my busy work life. I would often find myself turning into a robot, giving all of my un-centred self to others and producing like a mindless machine. I would lose all sight and awareness of the beauty of alignment and be left feeling empty and lost.

My biggest challenge was remembering to stay centred whilst in the midst of a high powered, high stress job. I would arrive at work, plug into my computer, blink, and it would be lunch time. Blink again and the time would be edging on 5pm. That's when the fatigue would set in and I'd realise that 97% of my day was full of go – go – go and I hadn't even given a second thought to my needs. Adrian's challenge led me to devise a solution that could integrate into my busy work day.

> **I programmed my most demanding business tool, my mobile phone, into my 'Alignment Ally'. Using the phone alarm feature, I set an alarm to ring every hour on the hour from 7am to 7pm each and every day with a simple reminder message attached to the bells – "Where are you?"**

Initially it took some time to become accustomed to the disruption of an alarm in the middle of my tasks. It was frustrating. As if I didn't have enough to do already and to then be disrupted by an alarm! I came to realise that it was my own mentality holding me back from being a full person; it was a resistant reaction from my lost un-centred self. I was ignoring my needs, giving all of my energy to others and defending that pattern with anger and resentment. In spite of this with help from my better judgement, I began to allow the process. I started with simple baby steps by taking thirty seconds to a minute to ask myself the questions – "Where Am 'I' Right Now – mentally, emotionally, physically and spiritually? What do I need Right Now? Do I need a coffee, a snack, a stretch, a walk, a quick meditation or a few breaths? What do I really need in this moment? The process started to incite some critical thinking towards the hardest of all the issues in my life; ideas about how to take care of myself. It felt good. Initially, just to stop for a few moments to take a few deep breaths was invigorating and energizing. I realised quickly too, that the process was much more powerful when I allowed myself to truly cut off from my tasks at hand, and dedicate as much of myself as possible to the simple process.

Where Am 'I' Right Now?

The more I allowed the process in, the more I started to respect the alarm reminders. It felt so good to take that small time to catch my breath every hour and to remember that I am actually a person with needs. So too, that deep inside I was actually wanting to set out to do things of value with my life. My dreams, my ambitions, my fire for life, had always been put on the back burner. Adrian's process fostered an opportunity for me to bring the real and positive aspects of myself into alignment and then start turning them into my ultimate goals – a complete paradigm shift. Keeping my dreams as my goals at the forefront of my mind, it started to make all of the previously aimless hard work worth something. The process also started to give me the faith in myself that I needed to believe that my road ahead was actually paved with love and joy. Isn't that what life is all about after all? Now that's my higher-self talking!

New insights gave me new sense of understanding that I was not a victim in my life. I was not a victim of circumstance, but rather that I was, and am, the creator of my own experience. I am responsible, I am powerful, and I am powerful because I am responsible for my life.

> **Checking in every hour on the hour became so successful, that over time I voluntarily shortened the intervals of the alarms to every half an hour.**

Having the consistent reminders, I allowed myself to feel good more often and I reminded myself not to submit my whole body and whole life force aimlessly into my work. I was choosing to take control of the energy I had to invest, and also to keep at the forefront of my mind a reminder that I was in control of the choices in my life. I discovered great love and care amongst my family and friends, and I began to work on developing those connections with positive intent and focus.

My dreams and goals grew to a new dimension as I aligned them alongside those of my loved ones. I realised that my loved ones and I were actually working as a team to achieve beautiful things together, and the contribution I was making as a centred man in my own power gave them strength. In turn, their strength gave me strength, and not only strength, but passion. A passion to live life as the full person and spiritual being that I know I really am and I know I really want to be.

For me, now, maintaining a high level of loving connection between my family and my friends has become of paramount importance in my life. I seek to love, connect, grow and contribute and I challenge myself to remain aware almost every moment of every day. Checking in and connecting with myself consistently has raised my level of awareness to new and beautiful heights. Work has now become a gratifying, neutral and non-tumultuous vessel for me to get from A to B financially, but ultimately it's only a finite commitment of my time and energy; a single aspect of the greater more wonderful whole that is my life.

When I still had a need for the alarms, I got to a point where I would look forward to them ringing. I started to want to become aware of myself and my feelings at the various levels of my emotional, mental, physical and spiritual misalignment – simply because it felt good to align them!

Over time, as the practice became habitual, I would remind myself like second nature of the importance of remaining centred. This was the beginning of meaningful positive self-talk, new found self-confidence and a realization of great personal power. "I am not just a mindless drone! I am important! There is so much more to life than this moment!" I would say to myself.

Where Am 'I' Right Now?

Nowadays, I have no need for consistent hourly or half hourly alarm reminders in my day to day life. Adrian's process was a powerful lesson in awareness. From a place of awareness, I have developed a strong sense of personal power which has, in turn, led me to make more enlightened and positive choices in my life. Using the Where Am 'I' Right Now? process was a bridge from an old way of thinking and being that was not serving me, to a new lease of life, to where I now see my future as a blank canvas ready to be filled with creation and love. I see my road ahead paved with love and joy, and it's truly remarkable.

Thank you Adrian my dear friend – Carlos

In early 2014, Carlos set up his own Real Estate Company (Up4Rent.com) and is doing very well with it. He continues to practice the Where Am 'I' *Right Now?* process and challenge himself to move up into higher levels of conscious awareness.

I would like to share a true story with you about David (not his real name) and how we worked together on the four aspects of the physical, emotional, mental and spiritual.

I was seeing David about an issue around him taking time out for himself and trying to build himself back up again after having a few life challenges which really took the wind out of his sails.

As we worked together with a process of him coming to see the different roles or identities that he was playing out in his life, we uncovered one aspect or personality within him which responded and acted strongly in the physical and spiritual realms but was not so very present or strong in the emotional and mental realms of his life. In different situations, another part of him was present and strong emotionally and mentally, but not so strong physically and spiritually.

After uncovering and acknowledging this pattern we worked on integrating him into one whole and complete person so that he could step into any future situations and be more present and empowered and whole. In this process David discovered that from being in a place of choosing to be fully integrated he was more centred, energized and aware and was more able to make clearer and more conscious decisions.

It is not uncommon for me to work with two or more aspects of a person's personality in my work as a coach and counsellor and to think of this as anything but normal is, in my humble opinion – plain crazy. We all have many identities and sides to our being. We wear many masks and play out many different roles and scenarios each and every day of our lives!

As you explore and work on evaluating and evolving your own physical, emotional, mental and spiritual aspects, see if you can determine which aspects in you are predominantly strong or weak. Perhaps you can explore and identify what happens to the different personalities within you when you are in certain situations. To remain fully integrated in these four realms of the physical, emotional, mental and spiritual takes a lot of practice and commitment, which you will discover as you work through this book.

We are much more than just physical beings; essentially we are spiritual-energy beings having an earthly experience. When we can grasp this and bring ourselves into alignment with this understanding, belief or knowledge we can then step into understanding ourselves from a more holistic and spiritual perspective.

Chapter Two

Understanding Ourselves from a Holistic and Spiritual Perspective

Studying and working with Anthroposophy and the work of Rudolf Steiner for over twenty years has given me a very clear language and context for my work and it gives me a safe and secure anchor point for my own spiritual investigation. I strongly believe that good solid preparation is essential when embarking on a journey of personal and spiritual investigation.

The four aspects of the human being, the physical, emotional, mental and spiritual, are probably not a new image or concept to you. However, the way in which I discuss, write or portray them may be different from what you already know or understand. If my language and descriptions are not familiar to you, or if they do not fit with your own language and terminology, please take the time to make it work for you so that you can allow the information in. When our old patterns of resistance, fear, doubt or ego come into play we often fail to connect with what is being offered and this can lead to us missing out on some useful, interesting or sometimes essential information. I would urge you to clear this up right from the very beginning so that you are more open to letting in what I have to share with you.

The Four-Fold Human Being

The four-fold model of the human being that I use in my work and wish to share with you was developed by Rudolf Steiner from his understanding and perspective of the spiritual human being from his own study and investigation which was built on earlier work from such great men as Socrates and Goethe. This model consists of the physical body, etheric body (or life body), the astral body and the 'I'.[1]

When we observe and recognise the human being as a 'whole' being, consisting of something more than just a physical body, then these four bodies can be seen, in a sense, to be operating as a complete integrated body. As we become more aware of these four aspects of ourselves we can then begin to take more control and responsibility for the way in which we live our lives.

> **In the Temple of Delphi in Athens are the ancient words:**
>
> *'Oh, man, know thyself and thou shall know the Universe and the Gods!'*

Our Physical Body

Our *physical body* – bones, skin, hair, nails, etc; are connected to the *mineral* realm of calcium, silicates, carbon and other physical elements. We can relate this to the idea or image of being 'earthly' beings connected to the Earth.

Pinch yourself a few times on your arms and legs and you will experience and know that you are a physical being. Do it hard enough and you will also experience and know the sense of pain!

This physical aspect of our being is what conventional health and medical practitioners generally work with. In alternative,

---

[1] If you are interested in gaining more knowledge about anthroposophy, I would highly recommend that you read *Theosophy* by Rudolf Steiner. Although it is quite esoteric, Steiner gives an in-depth and interesting perspective. The Barbara-Ann Brennan books: *Hands of Light* and *Light Emerging* are also interesting books to read.

complementary or holistic health and medicine other aspects of the human being are also taken into consideration, such as a person's soul and spirit.

I have heard people speak many times about their physical ailments returning again and again, even after treating them for weeks or even months or years. If practitioners, doctors or medical staff spent more time and energy investigating the emotional and spiritual connections within, around, or behind the ailment or illness, they may experience much better and more favourable results.

Let me make this a bit clearer. In this example I will use the analogy of the body being built up like simple building blocks:

For the purpose of this explanation, let us agree for a moment that we, as humans, have our 'I' (more on the 'I' coming soon) at the top of this building block system. We then have, below the 'I', an astral body (more on the astral also coming soon) which holds our emotions. From here our emotions come alive and from where our habits and addictions are formed and played out. We then move down and have the etheric or life body which sustains and keeps us alive and stores all of our life experiences and habits. If anything is out of alignment in any of these areas a process of 'contracting down' develops and ultimately the issue or the symptom can end up in the physical body as a physical ailment.

'I'

Astral Body

Etheric Body

Physical Body

If we are not fully in our 'I' presence and are struggling to stay centred we more automatically contract into the astral body which then becomes the dominant ruler of our experience or behaviour. It (the astral) becomes the boss!

If our astral body is out of alignment and running rampant, (which will happen if the 'I' is not present), then the emotional turmoil and residue from this untamed astral body has to go somewhere – and it does! This can impact on and damage the etheric body which then will have an impact on the physical body in some way.

Headaches, heart and kidney disease, liver dysfunction, gall stones and cancer, along with other physical ailments and diseases often have an emotional connection and as the whole body ('I', astral, etheric and physical) works somewhat like a filtering system, eventually it all gets stuck at the bottom – in our case, in the physical body! A good way to remember this is: 'The issue can get stuck inside the tissue!'

Here is an example:

If I was walking down a street and suddenly saw a snarling dog, which frightened me, my adrenalin would kick in – my instincts would take over and I would go into fight, flight or freeze mode. This is natural for us to do and generally we calm down soon afterwards thanks to our ability to produce insulin. If I remain fearful and anxious from this event, these emotions get stored in my being somewhere, especially if they are not dealt with. In the experience of a dog frightening me, if I continue to be fearful every time I see another dog in the street, it would start to have a deeper effect on me. If not dealt with, these types of experiences eventually get locked into our physical body somewhere; perhaps in one of our internal organs, perhaps somewhere in our gut. From this place there is nowhere else for the stuck emotion to go. It is the end of the filtering system. From here, major problems may, and often do, occur.

Can you see how the issue can get stuck in the tissue? It is like a filtering system in which we can, at times, forget to filter out the issue when it is stuck, thus leaving it to solidify and crystallize.

A useful image to help us understand this is the contacting or crystallization process of water which is made of one part oxygen and two parts hydrogen. Think of how H_2O goes from gas to steam, from steam to water and from water to ice. They all have the same basic ingredient or substance (H_2O), expressing itself in four different ways.

To stay in good health we really need to detoxify our emotions as well as taking care of our physical body. Can you imagine, for a moment, the build-up of toxins and the crystallization processes going on in our bodies if our emotions are not expressed or dealt with?

Annette Noontil, in her book *Barometer of the Soul*, gives some wonderful insights and possibilities of how different aspects of our being can become affected by certain emotions and life situations. Perhaps you can explore how some of your own physical ailments are connected to your own life situations or emotions. After many years of work in this field I no longer need convincing that our emotions play a big part in how we are doing physically. Good health and wellbeing is kept in order when we deal with all of our being, the physical, emotional, mental and spiritual.

We all step in and out of our 'whole-self' and in and out of our 'I' presence, many times a day. We contract and expand our bodies all the time. In the physical body, we do this through being hot and cold, relaxed and stressed or even by being happy or sad. When the physical body is injured or is in a state of dis-ease, it affects both the physical and etheric forces. The etheric body also expands or contracts depending on the situation that we find ourselves in during each moment of the day.

One way of understanding how the etheric body is connected to the physical body, is to understand that without our life force or life body (etheric body) we would be dead. The physical aspect is only one part of being human. It is the building, if you like, which houses the rest of our being. It is the container which holds the spirit and if our house is not solid and secure then we are more likely to be in a state of dis-ease.

The children's story of *The Three Little Pigs* depicts this very well. The wolf depicts the astral self, the shadow self or the double which can 'gobble us up'. The three little pigs represent the body, soul and spirit. It is when the three little pigs are all together as a whole and in a solid house that the wolf is outwitted and defeated. *The Three Billy Goats Gruff* story has a similar tale to tell. The meaning behind many of these old children's stories has been lost and/or misinterpreted over the years and it is wonderful to resurrect them to their truer meanings. As you read these stories again, you will perhaps see them in a different light with the knowledge and understanding of the four aspects of our being.

As our awareness grows we can learn to focus our attention and energy on our 'I' to be more in charge. This type of process is often referred to as centering, reconnecting to self or being in the Vortex[2]. Learning to bring oneself back into the present moment, back to one's centre, back to one's 'I', is a very powerful tool.

---

2   Esther & Jerry Hicks: The teachings of *Abraham*

Our Etheric/Life Body

Our 'etheric', or 'life body', is more connected to the plant realm, in an energetic sense. The plant world is made of the physical but also contains a living, measurable 'life force'. We can call this the life body. We can relate this to the idea of being like water beings – connected to the element of water.

This etheric body is somewhat like a mirror image of the physical body. The difference being, all of the separate parts in the physical body are represented and mirrored in the etheric body, as a whole, with no separation. The etheric body is a whole complete energy field. When our energy is low, holes or tears can appear in the etheric sheath or skin. Fortunately these holes and tears can be repaired and healed by using etheric healing techniques and by getting plenty of rest and sleep – sleep being one of the best remedies for replenishing our etheric body.

If we consider this and gain some deeper understanding of the etheric body, we can see that it is deeply connected with the realm of sleep. In essence, all plants live in a kind of dreamy sleep. They do not have the capacity to be 'awake' like animals or human beings do, because they do not possess an astral body. It is in this dreamy sleep realm where physical healing takes place; thanks to the etheric body. Sleep restores us energetically and physically each night. The physical body is in a constant process of decaying and dying and without the etheric life forces restoring us, mostly during night as we sleep, we would disintegrate very quickly.

Unfortunately, with most allopathic and conventional medicos, the etheric body is not even taken into consideration. When we are ill or do not attend to our needs it takes longer to recover and depleting the etheric forces through the use of certain medicines and medical practices and procedures may prolong the healing process.

The etheric body stores all our life experiences, along with our habits and addictions, on a cellular/energetic level. These stored memories of events and experiences in our lives, even if they are blocked out in our brain memory, can be successfully accessed and brought to light with the right therapeutic understanding and application. The emotional or astral orientated actions and reactions in our life are stored in the etheric memory body and remain there throughout our lives. By using psycho-therapeutic modalities such as those offered through Psychophonetics, these memories and experiences, if required, can be unblocked, transformed and healed. I use this knowledge and these tools in my counselling and psychotherapy work with clients who are working through 'old stuff' or addiction issues and I find that it is very effective.

The physical and etheric bodies cannot be separated. When they are, one thing is certain – death occurs! The etheric body *is* life; it *is* the permeating life force within us. It permeates the whole of our physical body and extends some centimetres outside our physical body. There is much literature and talk about people 'seeing' or experiencing energy fields and yes, they can be 'seen' or experienced by people who have the ability and/or the training to do so. With some practice, the etheric energy field can be observed, as can other energy fields. Just like any schooling, whether it is in mathematics, music or language, there is a starting point.

One way that people can learn to 'see' energy more easily is to spend time out in the realms of nature. With the correct training we can all learn to observe the health and vitality of a plant's etheric energy field.

For example, I was working with a group of year six school children at a Steiner School and was teaching them to observe the etheric energy field of leaves. I asked the children to take some time to look at the leaves in a certain way and then asked them to draw, as well as they could, what they had experienced. All ten children in the group had very similar colours and outlines in their sketches. They had all managed to 'see' and experience the etheric energy field in less than ten minutes of being shown how to do so.

If you would like to practice 'seeing' energy fields, you may wish to practice one or more of the following fun activities to give you a sense and understanding of how to do this:

1. Warm up your hands by rubbing them together for about thirty seconds and then hold your gaze along the edge of one hand. Focus your attention from the edge of your skin outwards to about ten or twenty millimetres. Keep your focus and look for a hazy or fuzzy light. As you practice you will begin to determine various colours in this fuzzy light.

2. Sit and focus on a candle flame and look just past the physical boundary of the flame. After some practice, you will see another set of colours beyond what you would ordinarily see. These fuzzy colours become more defined as you practice.

3. Look at a certain colour for a short while and then observe its counterpart colour – that is, the colour you see when staring at a white surface straight afterwards.

To do this, draw a solid red circle in your Where Am 'I' *Right Now* journal or on a blank piece of paper. Once you have done this, stare at it for about one minute and then quickly look at a blank white page or piece of paper. You will be amazed at what you see. If it does not work for you straight away, keep trying until you see a circle of a different colour. Try doing this with red, blue, yellow and other colours and see what happens.

Dowsing rods have been used for thousands of years to find water and underground minerals and have also been used to measure people's energy fields. When used correctly, pendulums can also do the same thing. It does not take long to learn how to use a pendulum or a set of dowsing rods and you can have lots of fun with them.

The pendulums I have been making for several years are created by collecting pine cones from a pine forest in NSW, after they have been stripped back to the core by cockatoos. It is this core which I make into a pendulum. By inserting a small Vortex energy card[3] inside the pendulum it adds an energetic field within and around it, making them super sensitive. For more information on Vortex energy cards and pendulums see the information at the back of the book.

Our Astral Body

Our 'astral body' is imbued with individual soul aspects or bodies of which there are several[4]. The astral body is more connected to the animal realm in the sense that animals have feelings, instincts and

---

3   These Vortex energy cards are designed and created by Jeff Levin, the founder of Life Alignment.

4   In Anthroposophy these soul aspects are called the Sentient Soul, the Intellectual Soul or Mind Soul and the Consciousness Soul. Each of these soul qualities are expanded as we work on our soul development. For more information read Theosophy by Rudolf Steiner.

natural habits and drives like mating, eating and migrating. Like plants, animals are also made up of the physical and etheric, but they also have this other dimension called the astral body. For humans, having an astral body means that we can experience feelings, desires, instincts and emotions.

With some preparation and insight, (because we have an 'I') we can learn and choose to over-ride or transform our astrality. With some work, we can transform our more negative behaviours into something more conscious and controlled. Rudolf Steiner called this tamed astrality – Spirit-Self. We can use our imagination and try to visualize an image of transforming our untamed astrality into Spirit Self. As we move through the book, this image will become much clearer.

Ultimately it is this Spirit-Self that we are trying to become in our journey of personal-spiritual development. If we hold this vision and come to some conscious understanding of what it is that we are trying to reach and attain, it can make it a lot less confusing and give us a much clearer sense of why we embark on such journeys in the first place.

The 'I'

The core aspect of our being, referred to throughout this book as the 'I', can be a challenge to really grasp and fully understand. The various religious, spiritual and psycho-analytical terms and meanings can become very overwhelming and confusing. The 'I' that I refer to is from my understanding and study from Anthroposophy.

> *"The 'I' lives in the body and the soul,*
> *but the spirit lives in the 'I'"*[5]

---

5   Steiner, in *Theosophy*

The following information will help you to understand this more fully.

Our 'I' is fuelled by spirit. It is imbued with spiritual energy and light. The 'I' is the core essence of our being and is, or certainly should be, in charge.

Of all the physical beings on the planet, only the human being has an 'I'. It is this very aspect of our being which allows us to act out of moral free choice – or not! By possessing an 'I' we can become self-conscious and conscious of others. A big part of humanities problems arise when people do not have a very awake 'I' and are directed through their astrality and are not self-conscious or conscious of others. Much of what I see and experience with many of the current spiritual teachings is not so much that it is spiritual, but that it is more astrally orientated; often with the mis-guided belief that it is spiritual work.

Having been a drug user for many years, which is very much connected to the astral realm, and then having experienced spiritual realms through my spiritual investigations for over twenty years, I have experienced both worlds. Although they have similarities in that they are beyond the physical realm, they are different in both their make-up and what they have to offer. One could say that the 'beings' of the astral realm play upon the senses of our mind and our emotions and feelings (like fear, doubt and hatred) whilst the spirit beings work with us for more exalted reasons. When doing any spiritual work this distinction becomes very important. I have witnessed and also helped many people overcome the negative and sometimes frightening effects of being involved with astral teachings and experiences and I myself steer very clear from anyone working in this realm.

Where Am 'I' Right Now?

It is always wise to check out the credentials of spiritual teachers and ask them where they were schooled and for how long and who their own teachers were. Safe guarding oneself against being taken on an astral mystery trip is well worth while and I would strongly advise that if you do decide to go off on some weekend spiritual enlightenment trip with someone, be well prepared for what might happen. The analogy that I often use is that you would not go scuba diving without first having lessons and going up into the astral or spiritual worlds is as colourful and dangerous as it is to go down into the ocean. It is wise to get some basic lessons first.

It is in the astral realm that our wishes and desires are formed and it is in the etheric body that our habits and addictions get lodged and stored from these desires. Through the engagement of the 'I' these habits and addictions can be changed or removed. When working therapeutically to support people with habits and addictions, it is the astral that the 'I' battles with. It is the astral that has the desire to keep the habits or the addictions – the etheric body is simply the store keeper.

While the astral body connects us to the element of air, the 'I' connects us to the element of fire – to the fire beings.

If we follow the history of humanity, we can see that we have become more and more 'individualized' with a growing tendency towards less group consciousness. Using our conscious spiritual 'I' is a major aspect of becoming and staying centred, being aware and able to make conscious choices. The 'gift' of the 'I' is that we do have the freedom of choice and can express our individuality. The question that we have to ask is – can we use this free choice responsibly and wisely?

The exercise about checking where you are *Right Now* demonstrates quite clearly how the process of becoming more conscious works. The 'one' who chooses to do the exercise and the 'one' who chooses to be centred in the wholeness of being *is* the 'I'.

Let us develop an image:

When we are caught up in our untamed astral behaviour, we each, with the strength of our 'I' have the choice and the ability to become more centred to pull ourselves up or out of any situation that we might find ourselves in. In these moments, it is our 'I' that awakens and takes action. If you are feeling down and depressed and swamped with astrality and suddenly find the energy to snap out of it or do something creative, this is the 'I' becoming more present in your being. It can take quite a lot of work for people to learn how to lift themselves from feeling depressed, but with some good therapeutic support and guidance, it can be achieved. Experience as a therapist has shown me that depression is not just a clinical condition but also a condition of the soul.

By doing the exercises offered in this book we can become more aware of our 'I' and the choices that we make. Let us entertain the idea for a moment that 'joy' is the most natural expression and condition for us (which I believe it is) and all other expressions and conditions are signs and symptoms of something being out of balance.

Imagine how life would be if we all held this view and used it as a platform for all of our thoughts, feelings and actions. Wow, we could start The Joy Club. Does anyone want to sign up?

Another interesting fact is that when we sleep at night our fourfoldness changes. This happens so that the etheric/life body has time to replenish and restore the physical body. The etheric body cannot really do its restorative work completely when there is busy astral activity. The astral body and the 'I' have to separate from the etheric and physical bodies for this restorative work to take place. The astral body as such, aids the process of decay and dying while the etheric body works in the opposite way to help restore and build up our physical bodies. If we do not restore and replenish ourselves in a healthy way, with good sleep, good food and good healthy lifestyles, then the astrality will overcome and overpower us and start to wear down our physical and etheric forces more quickly. The astral body is strengthened as the etheric body weakens.

Once we can sense the nature and power of our astral soul forces and begin to more fully understand how it can become rampant in the first place, then we can begin to have some empathy for the many teenagers who struggle through their teenage years as they adjust to wearing and getting used to their newly developing astral body. It is like getting used to wearing a new pair of shoes which do not fit quite right; except for some, the astral body is at least a hundred times more uncomfortable.

We are born, by varying degrees, with the physical, etheric, astral and 'I' already within us. We are born with a strong physical presence that is cloaked in a mantle of etheric energy, partly our own, but mainly from our mother as her etheric energy field envelopes and protects us. The etheric body is what sustains and allows us to continue to be healthy and not decay too rapidly. This etheric body is with us continually throughout our life until we die. We live in our mother's etheric energy as babies and as young children up to the age of around seven years. We then begin to develop a much more independent etheric body of our own. From birth until about the age of seven years, the growing child's development is all about building up the physical body. From puberty, the astral body begins to develop more strongly and with some teenagers this is very noticeable. Everything in the teenager wants out. His/her whole body wants to explode. Just look at their skin, their emotions, their interests and their wonderful ability to press their parent's buttons by being out to challenge us!

Of course we are also born with a sense of the 'I', but it is not until around the age of around two-three years old that you will generally observe it in a child. When their independence is first really observed you will notice the child saying 'I' instead of 'me'. However, the timing of this may be different for some children as I know of a young girl who was saying 'I' from about eighteen months old, with strong definite statements such as: "*I do it*" and "*I do it myself.*"

I distinctly remember two occasions observing my own children birthing their 'I' statements. My third son, at about the age of three, suddenly stood up one morning in the middle of the living room with his hands in the air and said "*I am Oliver*". A few years later, when my daughter was about the same age, she was sitting in bed between me and my wife when suddenly she said, "*I am between Mummy and Daddy*".

Around about the age of twenty one the 'I' has generally almost fully arrived and ready to be expressed; allowing the full expression of our individuality to shine. The age of twenty one is still regarded in many cultures as the age of becoming an adult – the age of being independent.

One thing to understand is the challenge that the 'I' has in fully engaging and shining when our astral forces become rampant and strong, especially if it is strengthened by the use of alcohol, drugs, pornography or other addictive and destructive things. This is very noticeable when we observe the behaviour of people who have, and live with (unconscious) habits or addictions. When engaging in a journey of overcoming addiction, 'a battle' between the 'I' and the astral forces takes place. With some good supportive therapeutic work, the strong astral forces can be squeezed out of the driving seat by the 'I'.

The healthier we are as young adults, the easier it is for the 'I' to incarnate. If our astral body is fed with its desire for drugs, alcohol, pornography or other unhealthy habits or substances, then the astral forces may predominate over the 'I', slowing or retarding the development of the 'I'. This is the basis of my work – encouraging and supporting the 'I' to be more fully present so that each person can be consciously in charge of their life. I work with many people whose 'I' is not fully present because of their past or current lifestyle choices which have suppressed the development of their 'I'. Trauma, abuse and neglect are some ways which can hinder the 'I' in its development and it can take quite a lot of work to support someone to be fully present in their body after being 'out of it' for so long.

In the Men's Groups that I facilitate, I find there are many men who struggle to be present. Sometimes it appears like I am working with a group of forty year old adolescents. When I express this to men, they really get the picture that they are still controlled by their astrality and still stuck in their teenage or adolescent development stage.

A brief outline of the development process for the four bodies:

0 - 7 the physical body is developing

7 - 14 the etheric body is developing

14 - 21 the astral body is developing

21 - 42 the 'I' is more present and is developing

In our human-spiritual development, we begin with the growth and maturity of the physical body right through to the age of around twenty one years. From about twenty one, we then have the growth and the development of our psychological maturity through our soul capacities until about the age of forty two. For the rest of our life we then have the potential for the growth of our spiritual maturity. Of course, this is only a guideline, as we all mature and develop at different ages, times, stages and levels in our lives.

Having this life map of how we develop physically, emotionally, mentally and spiritually supports my work and has become a valuable tool. Recently I saw a client who was struggling with issues of past abuse. He was so locked into the identity and story that his psychological, emotional and spiritual growth had slowed and was not well developed. He was in his thirties. He was still being driven along by his younger self. After an hour or so into a counselling session, he was able to see and experience a sense of his present self as a more fully integrated person. After working with him for a while to help him develop his 'I' presence, he was able to stand and see his old self and take charge and make new, more conscious and more positive decisions.

A useful practice is to take some time out to reflect on your own life and to see if your developmental behaviour matches your current age – reflecting and evaluating your life journey, your own biography[6]. When you become more in tune and aware of this process you will begin to see and experience many more adults acting like adolescents. Warning – it's a bit scary once you really begin to see this, especially in yourself!

After many years of observing human behaviour, I have come

---

6   *The Human Life,* by George and Gisela O'Neil gives an informative and eye-opening explanation of human development. There is also a detailed life map included with the book which can be used to map your own life journey.

to the sad conclusion and realization that most of the general population live in a way that is not very conscious and live in a way that is very full of fear, doubt and lack of self-love. This statement and observation can be easily verified by simply opening your eyes and looking around you (perhaps from outside of your own harmony bubble if you are lucky enough to live in one).

Take a moment now to measure your own lifestyle and see for yourself what you may have to do to bring about a more healthy balance into your life.

If you want to improve and maintain your own etheric, astral and spiritual forces you could start by eating healthier food, drinking lots more good water, doing more meditation and having plenty of sleep, fresh air and exercise. You could also study and work with what I call 'The Six Degrees of Consciousness Development'. This will help you to move out of any old paradigms that you are stuck in and help you to step into a new and more conscious place.

Chapter Three

The Six Degrees of Conscious Development

Attaining new levels of consciousness is no walk in the park and how high your attainment is will depend very much on how much of your time, energy and focus you are willing to give. Yes, it takes effort, time, commitment and energy to move up to new degrees of consciousness and sometime it can be a hard slog. Attaining any new level of consciousness will depend firstly on you exploring, discovering and owning your current level of consciousness. You can begin this exploration by asking yourself – Where Am 'I' *Right Now* as a consciously aware person?

So that you can get a clearer understanding of this, I would like to give you an outline of these six degrees of consciousness. You can then assess for yourself which level or degree you believe that you are in and can then decide where to focus your attention to help you to move up to a new (higher) degree of consciousness. You may get a sense that you are between two stages and in the process of moving from one level to another. This is just fine and quite common. Just acknowledge for yourself where you are in this self-evaluation. You may decide that you are already way up in the top degree and have no need to enter into this. If this is really true for you – well done! However, as this book is about challenging you to be more fully in your 'I' presence, I would still like to positively challenge you to take yourself through the process to check it out to be really sure that what you think and what you do are in alignment. If you are already in your 'I' presence you will not mind doing it and if you find that you are not, you will gain some insights. Either way it is a win-win situation all round with nothing to lose and lots to gain.

I developed the six degrees of consciousness model from studying and comparing other models and from my own study and investigation into conscious development. See if you can identify the degree of consciousness that best describes where you are *Right Now*.

> **Remember**
>
> **This is not a judgement of who you are, it is just an acknowledgement of where you are *Right Now!***

This is simply a guide, an evaluation and an exercise to support you on your journey of furthering and deepening your consciousness. From this place of knowing you can evaluate where you are *Right Now* and look forward to taking the next steps of improving and positively changing your life.

So, let me explain what I mean by conscious awareness, so that I do not confuse or offend you.

If you take a moment to look at the world and observe what is happening around you *Right Now*, you will observe many beautiful and wonderful things. You will also be aware of things that do not fit into the realm of beautiful or 'good things', 'moral things', 'healthy things' 'intelligent things' or even 'wise things'. When we become more aware of these not so positive things going on around us and decide to stop engaging in them, or doing them ourselves, then we can say that we have lifted our conscious awareness.

We might for instance decide to stop smoking (which we know harms and kills), stop getting drunk (which we know causes many social problems), stop speeding in our cars (which we know adds to more accidents and deaths on the road) or we might change our negative behaviour towards people and deal with issues that we know are damaging, disruptive or just plain ridiculous. This is what I mean by raising our awareness. I have seen people throwing litter out of passing vehicles, fighting in the streets whilst drunk, abusing people because of the colour of their skin, eating food that is full of poisons (like most food in the supermarkets!), ... the list goes on and on ... You can probably write a long list for yourself.

And just to be clear, I have been guilty of some of these things myself and am always in the process of further developing my own conscious awareness. As I move through my life and look back at all of the crazy, un-moral, un-intelligent and harmful things that I have done, it makes me shudder. I was not always such a pleasant and nice man. I have a history like everyone else and from that I have some old residue (a nice word for shit) that still needs to be cleaned up. I am constantly in the process of cleaning it up and as I work towards my own deeper conscious awareness, I can become much clearer on what I wish to have in my life and how I wish to act. I am not perfect and have much to learn, but I know where I have come from and am proud to have moved way up the consciousness scale. You can read my personal story later towards the back of the book.

I developed and use this six degree model because I believe that it is not incompetence that keeps people from climbing the ladder of conscious awareness, but from not being educated, shown, offered or given the opportunity to do so. It is by offering people an understanding through educational exercises and skills (like the ones in this book) that will help people to stand more solidly in their 'I' presence. I believe that the main reason people are 'asleep' in their conscious awareness and development, is because they do not generally know any difference – they often do not even know that they are asleep! They have not had the chance or been shown, told, or given any opportunity, direction or indication of how to do this.

This is why this book has been written; to support, encourage and even challenge people to step up into a new level of conscious awareness so that they can choose to live a healthier and more fulfilling life; physically, emotionally, mentally and spiritually. As I am continually expressing to people; by engaging in personal development work it helps and serve you, your family, your community and the planet. Our defunct and out of date education system and the lack of personal and spiritual development programs within it, continually keep people from expanding their consciousness. Add to this the escalating use of drugs, (both recreational and prescribed) and the poor diets that add little or no nutritional value and you can easily get to see (with a little bit of conscious awareness) why much of the population is asleep. Compound this with T.V. advertising, electromagnetic and geopathic stress and stresses at work, in relationships and with the constant attack on the sensory system with fear and doubt campaigns in the media and it all becomes very apparent how challenging and difficult it is to stay centred and in our 'I' presence. I would almost go as far as saying that many people on the planet today are severely comatosed.

If people had some real education on how to live in the world with real life skills programs that highlighted and offered insights and understandings on the effects and damage that certain things have on them, then perhaps we would have a much better planet. As long as people are numbed down, as I have suggested, and kept in the dark and not offered or given this new kind of education, they will struggle to move up the ladder of conscious awareness and understanding, unless of course they have the good fortune or the will to seek and find it for themselves – perhaps even by reading this book!

Oftentimes, the easy way out for people (without perhaps even consciously doing so) is to pop a pill, turn on the TV, get stoned or drunk or get caught up in pornography, gambling or some other addiction and stay switched off. This seems such a sad and wasteful way to live and yet millions of people across the planet live this existence every day. With just a little bit more focused leadership from a few more consciously aware people the planet could really change and become a much more positive and rich place. As we do not have this conscious leadership from our main-stream political, religious or financial leaders, we will have to find other ways to access it.

When deciding to learn to do anything new, it is good practice to try and figure out and understand the information that is directing us towards our new learning. In many workplaces the four step model below is often adopted and used to give people some understanding and guidance of what the leaning process is. Read it for yourself and then decide if you fully understand it all. Oftentimes we read things once, let it get vaguely planted into our mind and then believe that we have a full understanding of it. To really fully grasp something we will sometimes have to study or observe it for some time, perhaps even reading or experiencing the same thing several times. I would encourage you to do this.

A commonly used four step model of learning

Unconscious Incompetence

Often described as not understanding what is going on and in a state of ignorance.

Conscious Incompetence

In this stage people recognise or admit their incompetence.

Conscious Competence

Understanding how to do something and doing it with an amount of concentration or focus.

Unconscious Competence

This comes from doing something in automatic after practicing the task over and over and performing it without having to focus on it.

This four step learning process is sometimes good to work with as it does describe a process of learning that is easy for most people to understand and follow. Even though they have parallels, these two models (the four step model and the six step model) are different in respect that my new model includes the 'I', which is the core element for being conscious. The four step model offers and highlights an understanding of a mental and psychological developmental process, whilst the six step model offers and highlights a more holistic approach and understanding to the learning process.

Let me explain this difference to make it a little clearer for you.

To explain what Unconscious Competence is in the four step model, it is often described by using analogies of rats or other animals being trained to do certain tasks that 'change' their behaviour. We are told that new habits are formed by repetitive actions, like cows on a dairy farm as they 'learn' to go into the dairy to be milked twice a day. When people are learning to do something and practice it over and over to get it more perfect, like students do at school to imbed knowledge ready for exams, they do not have to be very conscious of the process to re-member how to perform it over again and again. It becomes so imbedded in their being that they can almost do it in their sleep.

This process of learning is all well and good for some aspects of development but, as I have outlined already, it misses the key ingredient of working with the understanding of the 'I' which I am advocating as the key ingredient for conscious learning and development. To be clear, sometimes it is fine to be doing things in an unconscious or habitual manner, it just depends on what we are doing.

An example of this:

If I were living in Sydney and knew my way around I could drive my car in quite an unfocused and habitual way. I could drive much of the time out of time-formed habits (in my astral). Should I be a visitor to Sydney, I would need to engage my 'I' and be more focused and attentive to all that was going on.

Different situations in life call for different focuses and degrees of awareness and knowing these differences is very worthwhile.

The Six Degrees of Conscious Development

1. Unaware of being Unconscious

For people in this state of un-consciousness it is as if they are in a state of sleep or in some kind of coma. When people are in this state it is very often caused from the heavy use of narcotics/drugs, alcohol, pornography or some other form of addictive substance. It can often be the result of living with unhealthy diets or even from living with self-created fears and doubts or ones that have been inflicted or planted by others. This unconscious state may even have been caused by some kind of hypnosis or manipulation. Seeing someone in this state of being is often witnessed as if the person is living in an automatic or zombie like condition. In this state the 'I' is almost unable to shine. This is where your habits, addictions, actions or lifestyle are so out of balance that the 'I' is swamped and imprisoned and is unable to escape the bonds of the astral that bound it.

An example of someone who might be in this state of being might be of someone who has had their thoughts, feelings and emotions numbed with alcohol or drugs (recreational and/or prescribed) and/or someone who eats only junk food for most of his or her daily food intake. This type of person may spend their non-working time (if they are able to work at all) in front of the T.V. or computer watching mind-numbing and disturbing programs and movies that may include gross pornography or horror. The more of this type of mind numbing rubbish people watch, the more they close down and become numb and closed off to the world.

This type of person will have very little or no idea of his automatic and zombie like existence, he/she will resemble something like a robot, doing everything in automatic with little or almost no conscious awareness. Sadly, a person in this state of (un)consciousness would probably not be reading this book.

There used to be some 'graffiti' or 'wall art', depending on your perspective, on the way into Melbourne that I saw regularly as I travelled into the city by train. It said WORK – CONSUME – DIE. This sadly could sum up the characteristics and life of a person in this degree of consciousness.

There are many things that can keep us locked into this world of unconscious behaviour. Thankfully, for some people, they have an experience of something new, something that kindles the flame within. It awakens the 'I' into motion and then there is some real possibility of positive and creative change. As you can see from what I have written, this first level of (un)consciousness shapes a different image than that of the first level in the more commonly used, four step model. In this new six step it is not about a lack of understanding or about any ignorance that people have that keeps them in this level of (un)consciousness, it is about being numbed down by inner or external activities and influences.

It could be argued that this type of person has a choice, of stepping out of his or her situation, and yes, I agree with that on some level, but I am also of the opinion these days, as more information and experiences open to me, that people are sometimes 'taken' and/or 'held' in this lowest level of consciousness deliberately by other means other than by choice. I am speaking here about certain aspects of manipulation, deception and mind-control that I believe are being used to take and hold people in this realm. This is a whole subject in its self and can be further researched by anyone wishing to go down that rabbit hole.

2. An awareness of being Unconscious

Arriving at or being in this state of consciousness is like experiencing a first awakening. It is like having the first inkling that there is something else going on around you. It is like experiencing a light going on for the first time bringing you out of the darkness. This experience may arise from something that someone has said to you or from something that you observed, felt or experienced. Picture this as the 'I' cracking open the egg of curiosity and consciousness.

I know a man who read the book series *The Ringing Cedars*, better known as The *Anastasia* series by Vladimir Meagre. Reading these books kindled his flickering flame and piqued his interest in things more esoteric and spiritual. He has, in his own words, awakened from his slumber to being more wide awake in the world. He is now becoming much more aware of his 'Potential Self' and opening up to many new possibilities in his life.

Arriving at this first awakening stage of consciousness is akin to opening your eyes in the morning after a long night of dreams, or perhaps nightmares, and gazing into the morning light and not quite being sure of where you are or what is going on. It is like the moment just before gaining the awareness that you are awake and being alive and in your own bed. In this degree of consciousness you may have moments of confusion. It may feel as if you are slipping in and out of two different realities. This can be a confusing time for people and it is here that people often opt for some kind of medication, such as anti-depressants, to see them through. Although some forms of medication can be useful, in my experience from working with hundreds of clients in this state of consciousness, I believe that it can also keep them numbed down and stuck.

There is a wonderful film starring Jim Carey, which, for me, expresses this waking up stage very well. The movie is called *The Truman Show*. It tells the story of a man who has been manipulated into believing that he is living a certain life, when in fact he is just a commodity, just a product of a corporation that uses him in a live to air T.V. series. He is unaware of this until he begins to wake up through various events that take place around him. Another movie that expresses this well is a movie called *The Stepford Wives*, where the wives in a particular town all have robotic set habits and features.

If you open your eyes and look around you it may surprise you how many people actually live in, or very close to being in this state of being. The more people who partake in mind altering and numbing activities, the more the world population heads towards a population of human unconsciousness.

3. Awakening to becoming Conscious

This stage is similar to the third stage of the four step model. In my six degrees model, this is the stage where new decisions can be made to step into living your life in a new way. During this degree of consciousness people start to think about doing something, like give up the habit of smoking, changing their diet, start to meditate or even realize that they are in the wrong relationship, job or town. In this degree of consciousness people may realize that things need to change, but will have yet put their thoughts and feelings into action. This is what I call the birthing of the Individual 'I'.

This is the realm that many people on their 'new path' of conscious awakening experience. Here people have this feeling from deep within that it is time to wake up. They know from somewhere deep within that it is time and they begin to stretch and yawn out of their slumber to be more awake.

In my work as a therapist and coach, I see many people like this and love to share this moment with them as they suddenly experience a need or urge to challenge the way that they have been leading their lives thus far. They express the wish to awaken to something new and it all becomes very exciting as they make their wish to stop smoking cigarettes or stop their drug habit or tackle their drinking problem. I have a secret inner celebration when I meet these people in my work and I get excited for them as I see their future potential banging loudly from within them, waiting to be released.

After many years of working with this process, I can now see with more clarity, that when I was a regular drug user I was very unconscious in the way that I lived my life. I was 'lucky' that I always had a spark of consciousness or inner guidance lying half dormant somewhere in my being that stopped me from falling right into that void of unconsciousness. I often joke (but also consider this as a serious matter) that my Guardian Angels worked overtime when I was a youth!

When I observe and meet people in this third stage of awakening, I am always in deep gratitude of my own life journey. I often spend a moment or two in deep reflection and gratitude of my own journey through the various degrees of consciousness. As I sit here and type away at the keyboard of my computer I can really honour myself for where I have arrived at in my life after all of the challenges that have been set before me. I have overcome the grip of addiction with nicotine, marijuana and other drugs, alcohol, gambling and pornography. I have overcome these, and many other challenges and now stand in a place of being in my 'I' presence more and more in my daily life. For the other times, when I am not fully in my 'I' presence, it is simply work in progress!

4. An awareness of being Conscious

Working with and in this degree of consciousness is often the most challenging. It is the stage where you become aware of your own being and aware that you are more than you once thought you were. It is at this stage that you get to see a glimpse of your true potential. This is where you will begin to take on more personal responsibility and make plans to change things in your life. This is where you will start to question your own morals, beliefs and actions and plan to do something constructive to change the situation. This is what I call 'engaging with your 'I' presence'. During this degree of consciousness you might find yourself seeking some professional guidance as you begin to recognise that others in the world can assist and support you. Allowing support in your lives can be a big challenge but also a big conscious awakening if you have previously shied away from it.

During this period you may seek out and find a spiritual path, a teacher or a master that gives you a foundation to stand on as you explore other aspects of life.

In the weekly Men's Circles that I facilitate, I sometimes meet men who have lived a very unconscious life, perhaps dealing with an addiction or an unhealthy habit of some description. The fact that they have turned up at the Men's Group gives me a pretty clear indication that they are currently in this degree of consciousness. They have started to question the way that they live their life and now want to change it and are actually doing this by seeking support. It is not that I want to put them in a box or judge them; it is just an awareness of where someone is in their current developmental stage. This is no different, for me, than acknowledging where a young child or a teenager is in their developmental stage in life. We are all developing in one way or another and I believe that it is good to be aware and honouring of our own, and other people's development. When we become more aware of this we can then stand in a much better position to support ourselves and other people; especially if we are therapists or educators.

5. Awakening to becoming Consciously Aware

This is an interesting stage of conscious development. In this degree of consciousness you will become more aware of not only your own physical, emotional, mental and spiritual changes but also that of other's around you. You will, as the heading suggests, awaken to becoming consciously aware. This awakening to your new awareness is about being open to everything that is going on around you on the outside as well as on the inside. I call this the 'straightening of the 'I'. This is where you will begin to actually do what needs to be done. This is the stage where you take action. This is where you actually start to stand up tall in the world and get noticed.

Rudolf Steiner gave us indications of not just five senses, but twelve. One of these senses is 'the sense of self' – another is 'the sense of other people' (from a soul level). In this fifth degree of consciousness these two senses become very much alive. I find that I have to be especially awake to these two senses when I am working with clients; to be aware of my own possible reactions, projections and judgements and to be in tune with where my client is with his or her feelings and emotions too.

In this stage of conscious development you might begin to align yourself with other people who are already at this stage of development. You will most likely experience people asking you to join them in their activities, initiatives and endeavours. This is where you will begin to recognise in others what you see in yourself. Likewise people will also recognise in you what they see in themselves. This alignment, this recognition is often referred to in spiritual or esoteric texts as 'recognizing other initiates'. I do not say this lightly. I say this with all due respect to where people are in their life journey and would add that at this stage of development it really is like an initiation. It really is a time to call a spade a spade and honour the process and the position that has transpired. By taking this viewpoint and honouring where I am in my own personal journey of conscious development I can inspire and join others who have also attained this degree of consciousness, this degree of initiation.

In this level of consciousness one can speak highly of oneself with less ego and self-importance whilst honouring oneself with a deep reverence. This may be a time to leave one particular social circle and join another in recognition of the changes that have been made. I know that at various times in my life, like when I stopped smoking and drinking I changed my social circles as the activities and people no longer served or suited me.

6. Being Consciously Aware

The difference between this final sixth stage of conscious awareness and the final forth step of the four step model is the final sixth step acknowledges and incorporates the presence of the 'I'. It offers an image of how you can become aware, not through the process of practice until it is perfect, but through a process of 'knowing' what you are doing as you do it. By being completely in our 'I' presence, we can 'know' what we are doing as we do it. For me this *is* conscious awareness.

When we are at this level or degree of consciousness we can choose do things beyond just by rote or habit. We can choose to operate on a higher, more conscious level. Reaching this sixth level is the ultimate goal for everyone on the personal or spiritual journey. There are many names for it but ultimately we are all striving to get to the same place – a place of conscious awareness. This is the reward for all the hard work, devotion and challenges that we put ourselves through. This is where, to coin a phrase, it – just is. This is where the trying stops. This is the place that you arrive at when you become the master of your life. This is where decisions can be made that are fully conscious and where actions are taken that are in yours and other's best interest. Being at this degree of consciousness is being absolutely upright and fully aware of the inner and outer worlds and fully in your 'I' presence. If you like, you could say that from this place you are working with your sixth sense. At this level, at this sixth degree of consciousness, your sixth sense is truly open.

This sixth level is where I aim to be in most of my daily life. This sixth level of consciousness is where I challenge myself to be (from my fourth and fifth degree consciousness). From this place – I AM. There is no trying, guessing, failing, achieving, preaching, doubting or fearing, it simply – just is. In this place I am Master Adrian.

Look around you. Where are the people in these higher states of consciousness? Where are the men and women who inspire you and support you to be in this place yourself? Can you see them? Do you know them? Can you join them?

To help you clarify where you are and what this all means to you, make a list of the people in your life who you would call suitable role models. Who is it that you know that you would add to your list?

Doing this list will give you a bench mark from which to work from and give you a clear indication of where you are yourself on the consciousness scale.

Remember, this is not about judging or criticizing yourself or anyone else. This is about recognizing and honouring where you are *Right Now* on your own personal journey of conscious development. It is about acknowledging and owning what the current state of your consciousness is. You can be sure that other people will have their own judgements and opinions about where they think you are on the consciousness ladder. It does not really matter what other people's opinions or judgements about you are. As with all self-evaluation processes there are many aspects of ourselves that can be evaluated and I would like to make it clear that we all fluctuate from being a bit flat and unconscious in some areas of our lives to being more highly evolved in other areas at different times of our lives.

I know for myself that I fall short of being in the consciously aware department in some areas of my life and also recognise that I have times of being right up there in the sixth degree realm. Use this evaluation as a general indicator of where you are in your conscious life development and do not get too caught up about being in one degree or another. Like a thermometer, when you are contracted like an ice cube you will have less degrees of consciousness and when you stand more fully in your 'I' presence, basking in the warm bright (spiritual) light, you will have more degrees of consciousness. By degrees we move up the scale as we practice, practice and practice being a much better human being.

The idea of going up in degrees is not new – think of the Masonic Order and how members move up from being an apprentice (First Degree) right up to the highest degree of Masonry, all the way up to the 33rd Degree (Sovereign Grand Inspector General). Even at University you can earn a degree of some kind if you study and work at it.

The Six Degrees of Conscious Development model offered in this book is from my own investigation, study and creation and I trust that you will find it useful as you move onwards and upwards.

By being more conscious and awake we are generally open to further study to help stimulate our minds. One great thing to study is personality types and one set of personality types that I enjoy studying and working with come under the heading of The Four Temperaments.

Chapter Four

The Four Temperaments

Melancholic, Sanguine, Phlegmatic and Choleric

Like all other investigations of human spiritual development, the temperaments also need to be studied and worked with for some length of time and to some depth to be understood. The four temperaments are connected to the four elements of earth, air, water and fire. Our personal temperaments determine, to some degree, our characteristics and behaviour. Each temperament helps to determine our bodily shape, our moods and emotions and our tendencies in how we approach and do things in our lives. Not everything about the four temperaments can be covered in this one chapter so I would recommend that you read *The Four Temperaments* by Rudolf Steiner if you would like more information.

Each person is very individual and I feel that it is unhealthy and somewhat unwise to place people in too much of a box. Having said that, I believe that is good to understand people and what their make-up and personalities are so that we can engage and work with them more effectively. I would like to add that having any understanding, wisdom and knowledge about anyone should never be used in a manipulative or underhand way.

A few basic aspects of each temperament:

A person with a melancholic temperament is very often imbued with tendencies towards being inwardly focused and socially introverted. They may carry with them an air of sadness or foreboding. They may be someone who gives much time and attention to detail and perhaps an analytical thinker. People with a strong melancholic temperament are often thin with drooping shoulders and may have indrawn cheeks and even a sunken chest.

Sanguine people generally tend to be very social, colourfully dressed and talkative with a tall and thin body shape. They are often light on their toes. They may be inclined to be rather busy and perhaps scattered if they have not learnt the art of focus and stillness.

The phlegmatic type person will probably be more inclined to be a bit of a plodder or steady achiever; someone who is able to stick with a process and complete it. This person would generally be reliable and dependable to complete a task. Phlegmatic types can easily carry extra weight due to their watery constitution.

The choleric person is often a person with a fiery nature, with a tendency towards being in a leadership role. They can be a bit headstrong and self-centred on occasions if this fire is not kept in check. Choleric types are generally energetic and high energy people.

Each of us has a more prominent and dominant temperament which dictates and governs the way in which we think, feel and act and walk, talk and communicate in the world. The challenge, as always, is not to allow the more negative aspects of these governing energies to take control and lead us astray. This is why it is important for us to be forever vigilant in staying centred and in our 'I' presence. For people working with children or even adults, understanding the temperaments can be a useful resource as it gives us a way to communicate and interact with more awareness and can give us an opportunity to more fully understand and accept why someone might react or respond in a certain way.

Our body types or body shapes and the way in which we walk, talk, move and act in the world can give us some clues as to which of the four temperaments we are connected to. Once again, observation and attention are required to help us to become more aware of ourselves and other people. For example, I fit into the category of being predominantly choleric, with sanguine aspects as a very close second. Of course I also have aspects of being phlegmatic and melancholic in my nature but they are not as dominant as the choleric and sanguine aspects. To find more balance in my life I would do well to spend time with schooling and developing the phlegmatic and melancholic aspects and letting go of some of the more negative or non-serving traits that I carry as a choleric/sanguine.

The four temperaments not only link with the four elements of earth, air, water and fire, they also link to certain colours.

The temperament-element-colour connection

Melancholic – Earth – Blue

Sanguine – Air – Yellow

Phlegmatic – Water – Green

Choleric – Fire – Red

A fun thing to do is to paint these colours on paper and spend some time observing them to see how they affect you, especially your moods and emotions. When you do this, become aware of how each colour seeps into your being and note carefully what your reaction or response is to each one. You may also like to dress up in each of the four colours for a day or so and see how it affects you. When you start to become aware of the colour-temperament connection you may well start to notice the colours that people around you choose to wear. This may then give you an indication of their temperament. I have a standing joke with a good friend of mine David, about his choice of attire as he nearly always dresses himself in green and brown. I often jest with him about him being a true phlegmatic.

Colour therapy is a big area of healing and when used consciously it can help us to gain amazing insights and results. Each one of us will connect and react to colours in different ways and this is partly determined by our most dominant temperament. Personally I love red and yellow and once you get to know me it is not hard to work out my two dominant temperaments; and they are not phlegmatic and melancholic!

As you begin your journey of understanding and working with these temperaments you will experience many connections, such as the connection to the physical, etheric, astral and spiritual bodies that were presented earlier in the book.

Melancholic – Mineral world – Physical

Phlegmatic – Plant world – Etheric

Sanguine – Animal world – Astral

Choleric – Spirit world – the 'I'

Where Am 'I' Right Now?

If we are serious about empowering ourselves and becoming more conscious, it is good practice to observe ourselves and observe the way that we act in the world and go about our daily business. With this in mind, do you tend to go at things like a 'bull in a china shop' – choleric, or do you methodically, some might say plod, through your day – phlegmatic? Perhaps you find life a little tragic and difficult to cope with or perhaps you are you a deep, analytical thinker – melancholic? On the other hand, you may skit about during the day, going from one thing to another, like a butterfly – sanguine?

These are just general images for each temperament. Each one has many, many characteristics and of course we all have all four temperaments within us in varying degrees.

The choleric and the sanguine person will generally be more outgoing and extraverted in personality type whilst the melancholic and phlegmatic person will be more inclined to be inward and introverted.

Each of the four temperaments has their upside and positives, as well as their downsides and less than positive qualities. For instance, I can, if I'm not in a state of balance, become domineering, inconsiderate, sarcastic, angry, impatient and intolerant with my choleric nature – Just ask Arleen! When I am in a more present state of being, I can then stand more powerfully and positively in my choleric nature and become more productive, determined, optimistic and decisive, expressing positive and skilful leadership skills.

The more that we look at what is being brought to our attention, in terms of human spiritual development, the more we are able to see how everything is somehow connected.

Rudolf Steiner spoke of the temperaments as standing between two streams; the stream of our previous lifetimes and the stream of our hereditary or ancestral line. Having this description and image helps me to see where and what the temperaments mean to me. They show me quite clearly where they fit into my life. Knowing that the temperaments help to display and control the way that I am formed as an individual human being to some degree, helps me to acknowledge and then change aspects of myself in order to become more balanced and conscious in all that I do.

So, where are you, *Right Now,* in all of this information? Have you managed to form a more complete image of yourself? Can you identify which are the most dominant temperaments in your being?

Take some time now to create your own life map from all that you have learnt so far in this book. Spend some time writing in your journal about what you have learnt about yourself. See if you can create a clearer image of who you are and how you operate in the world. Knowing oneself is very empowering.

Write a few words about your current life situation, physically, emotionally, mentally and spiritually. Write something about your temperaments too and observe once again your connection to the colours.

Creating and working with self-evaluation in an honest and real way can help to bring us many new and useful insights and understandings about ourselves. If you give this exercise the time and energy that it deserves, you will be richly rewarded and will become much more self-empowered. It not only highlights the aspects of our being which may need to be further developed or changed, it also highlights our positive aspects and helps us to see and honour what we have already achieved. This is often quite a new and challenging realization for people who have not engaged in this type of work before. Honouring what we have got is empowering, even if it is sometimes challenging to accept.

> **Remember to keep asking yourself the question**
>
> *"Where Am 'I' Right Now?"*

When we learn to work with our personalities and our temperaments we can become much clearer on what makes us tick. We can then become much more focused on stepping into being someone who is more empowered and courageous and self-responsible. What this will also do for us is to help us end the dull and un-serving blame game that often keeps us from being fully empowered.

Chapter Five

Ending the Blame Game

One of the most powerful things that we can do on our journey of spiritual development is to start taking more responsibility for our actions and to stop blaming others. This exercise will support you to do this. As with all the exercises in the book, the more you choose to put in, the more insights and results you will receive back.

Think of a person with whom you have had a difficult time with in the past few days or weeks. Go on, there must be someone that has gotten under your skin. Now, imagine this person standing in front of you *Right Now*. As you imagine this person standing in front of you, recall the situation that you were in. See if you can see the whole picture from a bird's eye view. See yourself in the scenario too and use your imagination, memory and honesty to recall how you were in that moment, physically, emotionally, mentally and spiritually. How were your reactions, projections and judgements? Can you find it in you to own your part in the situation? Can you see that the fault or the blame was not all about them? Can you place yourself in that scenario again and recall how you played your part in it all?

Where Am 'I' Right Now?

This exercise is one that I love to do for myself and I love hearing back from people that choose to take this exercise on. Time after time I get to hear that lives are changed for the better as people adopt and use it. It is especially good when couples use it to strengthen their relationships.

Using this empowering technique in everyday situations is often where and when it begins to dawn on us (if we have the courage and the desire to really experience it and step into our power), that we can begin to take more self-responsibility for our own thoughts, feelings and actions. We really can change things and stop the old blame games! Wow – imagine that! Imagine for a moment that you have the ability to stop blaming others. This is often a difficult concept for people to grasp. It is sometimes quite a challenge to change years of not taking responsibility and blaming others for the mistakes, difficulties, challenges, misfortunes and bad luck that has unfolded. When we finally take responsibility and stop blaming others, we can let governments, friends, families, partners, teachers and many other people off the hook. This is really empowering stuff – this is real freedom!

Let's continue the exercise. Keep the same scenario in your imagination and see if you can replay the scene in a new way. See if you can re-act or re-enact your part. See if you can find another, more positive way, to say, feel and do what you did previously. Act it as if you were out to get an Oscar award. Do it with absolute conviction.

Get a sense of how you are feeling *Right Now* after experiencing this with your new insights and understanding. Be aware of the two different scenarios and the way in which you were in each of them. When we choose to do these reviews and re-enactments on a regular basis we can become more aware of our own input and our own unconscious behaviour patterns.

When doing this exercise, always try to remember to apologize (even if only using visualization) to the person who you were just working with and let them go; let them off the hook, knowing that they were not to blame for the situation. When we become more fully empowered and more regularly and honestly own our own behaviour patterns we will get to see that almost always it is ourself that created the situations that we find ourselves in – yes, we actually do create our own reality!

When I am working with people who are caught up in the blame game in one way or another, I often have to spend quite some time on this subject with them to really bring it home to them. It is often very challenging for people to come to a position of ownership and self-responsibility as it is really saying to them – grow up and stop acting like a child or adolescent.

In the men's work that I do, I get to observe what a big step it is for some of the men to grasp this notion of growing up. Stepping from childhood to adolescence is one thing, stepping from adolescence into manhood is quite another! Challenging ourselves and stepping into a place of more responsibility so that we can grow and stop the blame game is very rewarding. Even though it can be difficult at first it is well worth persevering with and the more we practice this, the more we see the positive changes.

> **Build solid and strong relation-ships and you will sail a much steadier course through your life!**

As we sail through life we are met with many challenges and issues. They come towards us whether we like them or not. The real test is how we face and deal with each one of them. This is where the question of choice comes in. Every challenge or issue offers an opportunity for us to learn and become conscious of our

Where Am 'I' Right Now?

reactions and responses. How we deal with the situation, challenge or issue is generally dictated by how we are in our being – how we are physically, emotionally, mentally and spiritually. If we are out of sorts and not very centred, then the challenge or the issue can seem bigger than it actually is. If we do not remain centred we can very easily make mountains out of mole hills and become flustered, confused, angry, irritated, depressed or even ill.

One of the most common places where this 'blame game' gets played out is with couples. Because some of the most intimate, personal and sensitive issues are created in couples relationships, it is therefore not surprising that we get into blaming our partners for certain things that happen to us. If we are feeling a bit flat, a bit unhappy or frustrated it is easy to lay the blame onto our partner. Learning to not react and blame takes a lot of skill and is something that has to be practiced on an almost daily basis. Overcoming and learning how to stop the blame game is one of the most powerful and rewarding things that I believe couples can do to help take their relationship to new levels of intimacy, trust and consciousness.

I know for myself that when I am in blame mode and start to blame my wife for something that I perceive she has said or done, I lose a sense of power and my sense of personal responsibility. It is easy to blame others and much more challenging and difficult to realise and acknowledge that it is we, ourselves that we need to shine the spot-light on. I recommend that all couples put in some time and work if they wish to put an end to the blame game. In our Naked Truth couples work and retreats, Arleen and I work with this and find that for many couples it is both the most challenging and the most rewarding topic.

There are many places that we can go to too step into our work; in a studio with a therapist or coach, on a retreat or even into a weekend workshop space. One place that we can also choose to go to in order to reconnect with ourself is into the realms of nature. Here we can take the journey of self-discovery and self-realisation into a whole new space. In the nurturing space of nature we can connect psychology and ecology, nature and soul.

Chapter Six

Eco-Soul Bush Experience

Several years ago, whilst living in South Africa, I developed what I called Eco-Soul Bush Therapy (renamed in 2010 as Eco-Soul Bush Experience). It was developed, in part, whilst facilitating a series of personal development and Bio-Dynamics (BD) gardening and farming workshops where people were learning to connect with the earth and to the realms of nature in a much more meaningful and deep way. In these BD workshops, people were being guided to connect to the more subtle aspects of farming and gardening; to nature, the earth, the elements and the elemental beings.

I noticed that some people did not connect very easily, whilst others experienced deep emotional and spiritual connections. As I worked more and more with people on the land and in nature, I started to develop and implement more exercises to deepen these connections. By further exploring, understanding, and supporting people to transform and heal their emotional experiences the processes deepened and from this I created and developed Eco-Soul Bush Therapy/Experience. After leaving South Africa I developed the work further and now offer it as a one day experience for individuals, couples and groups with specific topics or processes to suit their needs.

The Eco-Soul Bush Experience is useful for people to explore, discover and understand themselves in more conscious ways with the support of nature. By spending a day in the realms of nature participants are guided and supported on a very engaging, empowering and powerful journey of exploration, discovery and transformation.

An Eco-Soul Bush Therapy Experience story from South Africa.

The following is an extract from a chapter I wrote:[7]

A group of people were taken into a beautiful arboretum outside of Cape Town, in South Africa, in the early spring of 2004. We spent some time adjusting to our new surroundings, our new environment, to our new skin. Each person is asked to go and find a tree to connect to and to spend some time with it, to begin some sort of dialogue with the tree and to get a picture of who and what the tree represents for them (from a metaphoric sense). After this, we gather again to share the experiences within the group.

The first person to share his experience describes in great detail how he experienced the emotional state of his chosen tree, the way it expresses itself through its shape, how it speaks and how it feels being in the arboretum. The tree is a mirror for him, and he is expressing his inner world with the tree being a mirror of his inner soul.

Another person introduces us to her experience of a tree. She had been sitting next to the trunk of a tree and gone into a meditation. She had an inner visual experience of running across an open plain, hunting with others and holding a spear in her hand. There was a group of hunters and she was part of it. She goes on to describe the scene in great detail. It is a very powerful picture of a tribal African hunt. When she finishes sharing her experience, she says that she is not feeling very happy as she had enjoyed being the powerful and

---

7   Hanks, A. Chapter 14: An Eco-Soul Bush Experience: Therapy in the Bush. In *Psychophonetics Holistic Counselling & Psychotherapy: Stories & Insights from Practice* by Robin Steele (ed), 2011: pages 239-240.

courageous hunter and now she is feeling weak and powerless. Her wish is – to be powerful and courageous in her life now.

The client's wish gives the counsellor and the client a direction for action. We discuss how to proceed, and we go to a small clearing to draw a large circle about four meters in diameter in the soft leaf-covered earth. Then we each pick up a thick stick just over a meter long and step into the circle. For the next ten minutes, we do not go out of the circle as we engage in a mock battle. The rest of the group sit outside the circle as witnesses. We move around in the circle until near the end of the time when she says that she feels like a warrior queen and expresses another wish – To be a Warrior Queen. She then tells the group how she needs to become more like a warrior in her life, to deal with all the stuff she has to deal with. Then she goes for a walk by herself to really feel and deepen this connection with the Warrior Queen quality.

While she is gone, the rest of the group start to make a crown for her from leaves, twine, bark and grasses. We also find a log for a throne, wood for a sceptre and mace, and we create a special area that is fit for a queen's coronation. When she returns she is asked if she can honour herself, and whether she has the strength to carry the queen quality inside. She says that she can and is feeling strong and queen-like. We rake back a big mound of leaves and she lies down on the earth. We cover her with the leaves and she lies there for several minutes. When she is ready, she rises out of the leaves and walks into the space we had created for her. There she is adorned with the crown, the sceptre and the mace. Together we create a sacred and personal ritual.

Follow-up:

A few weeks later, she reports that this day has been one of the biggest turning points in her life. She went to her father's house shortly afterward and healed some old wounds with him, which had been there for many years. She also had the courage to end a relationship that had previously been difficult to end.

One woman who experienced a day with an Eco-Soul Bush Experience in Australia shares her story.

I have felt I have been reasonably successful in life. I attended college to obtain a Diploma and entered the workforce upon graduation into my chosen field. Within two years I was receiving industry awards for my achievements and received an invite to work overseas in Houston, Texas, USA. By the age of twenty four I was running a subsidiary branch for the company I was working for. Two years later I relocated for a lifestyle change and by the age of twenty eight I was fully responsible for the running of a $20M business. These jobs have always provided extremely well financially for me.

At the age of thirty I didn't feel very successful. I was still single after a series of unsuccessful relationships, putting in my heart and soul for seemingly little return for my efforts. I wasn't satisfied with my job. Spending a lot of time away from home and selling products I no longer had any belief in. I began to think there was no purpose to life and if this is what it was about, I no longer wanted to be a part of it.

I found Adrian's business card in my diary – it seemingly came from nowhere as I am still unsure where I collected it from. I kept looking at it for a few weeks until I finally rang Adrian. He was very understanding and felt he could help me.

After years of corporate training on how to communicate I arrived in Byron Bay to see Adrian with the hope that maybe he could 'crack me'. I had my doubts. I had years of hiding my true self. I had seen a lot of psychologists, councillors, had years of company training and read numerous books on how to appear confident and handle my emotions. I had spent all of my life living someone else's dream, covering my true emotions, too scared to leave as I didn't know who I was or what I wanted to do. I was also very afraid of what everyone else might think of me. I was afraid I could also fool Adrian with this lie as well as I had myself and many others.

It was time for me to get real! Adrian reached in, grabbed my soul and taught me how to love myself. He was encouraging and understanding. He knew just how far to push me and he defiantly knew what buttons to push. It was a journey of self-discovery and self-love: Finding my heart space, my truth and my purpose.

Uncovering the layers of defence I had so successfully built over the years. Finding my inner child and all the younger versions of myself and teaching me how to love all of them – the past, the present, warts and all. It was extremely moving, empowering, a life changing experience.

I found my heart space and left knowing and understanding myself a lot better – an increase in self-love and self-respect. I found my centre and a connection with my soul.

This woman and many other people have experienced a day out in nature to explore, discover, transform and heal some of their challenges and issues. Each time I go out with anyone I am always filled with a sense of awe and gratitude for the amazing gifts nature brings and offers at the right moment for each person and situation.

Working out in nature, I find that the counselling, psychotherapy or coaching process that unfolds is richly supported and nurtured by the natural surroundings of nature. Some of the addiction work with clients is often undertaken outside with the support of nature, as I find being out in the fresh air and in the natural elements, heightens and intensifies the process and gives the clients a greater connection to their true, non-addicted, self.

Working out in nature is such an amazing experience and I just love that I can do this and get paid for it! Whenever I get the chance, or make the choice to go out into the bush, climb a mountain, walk on the beach, swim in the ocean, go out into the desert or just sit in my garden, I get a deep appreciation and connection and satisfaction. Taking people out into the realms of nature as a facilitator and therapist is very rewarding and I love to observe the sense of wonder and connection that people receive when they venture out. I am lucky to have David Styles as a friend and colleague, as he also facilitates outings into nature, so I not only get to facilitate others, but also experience being guided out in the realms of nature too.

David has created Deep Nature Connection and in addition to his live nature connection events, he has put together an amazing set of nature study DVD's, CD's and written material to help people connect with nature in a deeper way. David's earth wisdom is wonderful to tune into and it is both fun and educational to spend time with him out in nature on one of his or my nature events, or out finding hollow logs or being in my 'man-shed' creating hollow logs into didgeridoos. One of the exercises that I really enjoy with David is where he gets each person to tune into a specific thing, such as a bird, tree or animal, and sense and 'hear' what it is 'saying' to us. Listening to nature in this way can reveal and give us many wonderful moments, lessons, insights and answers if we choose to be open enough to listen.

David features in a couple of my Didgeridoo DVD's and is also in the Eco-Soul Bush Experience DVD that I have produced. It is set in the Australia bush and gives people the opportunity to see and

Where Am 'I' Right Now?

sense into what it is that I offer. Information on how to get this, and other DVD's, can be found on my website Please see the details at the back of the book.

As mentioned earlier in this chapter, one of the things that I do whilst out in nature, is to work with people to help them with their challenging habits and addictions. In this space, out in nature, deeper understandings and insights of what habits and addictions actually are can be revealed. Each and every one of us has some kind of 'bad' habit or addiction and having an understanding of this and learning to engage with the 'I' to help us overcome our habits and addictions is well worthwhile for all of us, whether we are therapists, parents, a partner to someone, or simply because we are a man or a woman dealing with our 'stuff'.

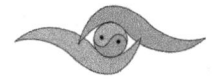

Chapter Seven

Habits and Addictions

In this chapter we will gain deeper insights and understandings into how to engage and work with our 'I' as a tool for helping to overcome and end (bad) habits and addictions.

As previously discussed, it is in the astral realm that our wishes and desires are formed and it is in the etheric that the habits (and addictions) get stored. It is through the engagement of the 'I' that these habits and addictions can be challenged, changed and removed. When working with clients on addiction issues my task is to help them to engage with their 'I' presence so that they can 'do battle' with their strong astral forces. It is the astral that has the desire to keep the habit or addiction alive and it will try every trick that it can conjure up to keep it alive. As a therapist I have to be able to guide, support and teach my clients how to 'out-smart' the astral with new tricks and skills. The etheric body has no part in this battle – it is simply the store keeper. However, etheric based therapies, such as etheric massage, can help to support the process.

Here is an example of how I work with people dealing with addiction:

One very simple and practical way in which I work with people with nicotine or marijuana addiction is to ask the person (the smoker) to stand a cigarette or joint/reefer up on its end in the middle of the room, or on the ground if working out in the bush. I then ask them to conjure up their sense of 'a higher-self' and get them to stand next to the cigarette or joint.

<u>Where Am 'I' Right Now?</u>

We spend a few moments comparing the size of the cigarette or joint both energetically and physically and describe together all that it stands for. We then look at the size of the person's energy (physical, emotional, mental and spiritual) as a comparison. It does not take the person very long to see the absurdity and/or hilarity of the situation. Whilst the person is standing and feeling their power, standing in their 'I' presence, the question is asked: Are you a smoker? The answer is always *"no"*. Having the person stand in his/her 'I' position and making this statement is one of the strongest motivational tools to support them to quit. In this space, they get the sense of standing in their 'I' presence, a powerful act for them. This moment is generally the end, or near end of smoking for the client. The battle is raged in a few minutes … The 'I' becomes the victor as he/she stands over and shrinks the addiction (the IT).

I have worked with many people in this way and I find that getting people to engage and work with their 'I' is the most empowering thing that they can do to support themselves through an addiction release process. When working in this way the person is fully conscious and can make informed and conscious decisions and learn to take full control of their decisions and actions. In this process there is no trickery, manipulation, coerciveness or hypnosis and there is no need for any substitute nicotine patches or e-cigarettes. The main thing to remember for this work is to fully engage with, and use, the 'I' as the conscious decision maker.

When Linda (not her real name) asked me to help her to give up smoking, she was already engaging her 'I' as she felt that smoking was no longer something that suited her on her new path of working with people as a healer. She wanted to give up but was not sure how to do it. She had tried several times before and had not managed to do so. We spent just ten minutes doing the 'Standing the Cigarette Up' exercise and she has never smoked again! Her 'I' presence was very strong and she made the commitment and the conviction to stop there and then. Disconnection and loss of our 'I' is a major factor with addition work and re-energising and re-connecting with the 'I' is an essential part of breaking the addictive patterns.

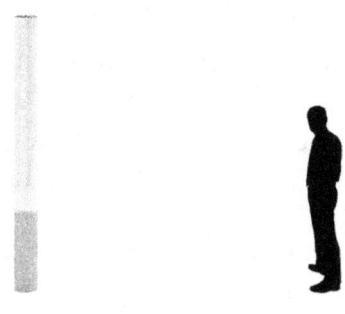

'IT' (the cigarette) and Little me

The picture above shows how a cigarette can seem larger than life and how the 'I' can be overshadowed and shrunk by IT.

'IT' and 'I'

In the picture above, we can see how the 'I' now overcomes and shrinks the IT.

When worked with more consciously and with a deeper understanding of human dynamics and behaviour, addiction work can have great results. With the correct understanding and knowledge and with a good application of therapeutic tools, such as the ones outlined here, the 'I' can be strengthened to overcome the addiction, thus giving the person a new sense of self-empowerment.

Sometimes, as with the case with Linda, the addiction can be over in a matter of minutes, whilst for others it can take a few days, weeks or even months to completely break the pattern. Depending on each circumstance and on the level of each person's wish to engage and change their situation, each addiction situation and story has its own time factor and this has to be honoured.

When working with any 'bad' habit or addiction, we have a choice. We can choose to be the 'little me' or the 'big 'I''. It really is a matter of choice. Yes, I fully accept that sometimes it can be a struggle and a challenge and that a battle has to take place between the 'I' and IT, but there is nearly always a choice to be free of the addiction.

When people are heavily swamped in their cloud of emotional astrality, it is often very difficult to see, feel, experience and live outside of this dark, often all-consuming cloud. When people are 'in' (the cloud) they remain stuck until they can get 'out'. These places of addiction can be very difficult places to get out of and that is why people may need to seek expert and professional support.

When we are not in our power and not standing in our 'I', it can seem like an impossible task to face IT and it may take some time to shift our habit or addiction. Sometimes it is a case of rolling up our sleeves, dressing in our strongest armour and doing battle, just like the image of St George overcoming the dragon.

When we stand in our centred being, we are then truly in a place of being awake, conscious and alert. In this place we can be more in charge of our reactions, projections and judgements and ultimately more in charge of our life. When we are fully in our 'I' presence, we are more able to clear the dark clouds away.

Habits and Addictions

The 'I 'emerging

Fully present 'I'

By overcoming and taming the dark cloud of addiction we become more in charge and in control of our thoughts, feelings and actions. By taming IT we can stand more in our strength, in our 'I' presence.

Where Am 'I' Right Now?

> **Remember: We tame IT – We do not destroy IT.**

By taming and not destroying the IT we really know that we are in charge. There may be times in our lives when we may like to use this 'other aspect' of our being – this IT.

Here is an example of this.

Inside of me, sits an old Punk Rocker from the 1980s who is not always a very pleasant person to be around, especially if there is a situation of conflict, like a fight in the street. It takes lot of energy and effort for me to keep the punk rocker tamed as the energy of the situation ignites old memories and actions within me.

However, if I am with my wife Arleen or one of my children, walking through a rough and dangerous part of Cape Town, South Africa, the punk rocker is welcome and is a good person to have around because he can protect them. The trick is to know when to express these 'other aspects' of ourselves and put them to good use. That is why we never destroy them; they might just be useful to us one day in the future.

See if you can develop an image of all the various characters living within you. We have many faces, personalities and different ways in which we act in the world and it is useful to know them. When we come to terms with the fact that there are many aspects of our being, we can then begin to more fully understand how various situations can get out of hand. We need to be aware if our 'I' is in charge or if another aspect of our being is in control. If we are not driving the bus, so to speak, then some other aspect of ourself is doing the driving and the 'I' becomes a back seat passenger – usually at the very back! When we are not being present in our 'I', life can becomes like a mystery tour, where we are not entirely clear about where we are going.

Habits and Addictions

Compile a list of the different characters within you. You can have some fun with this and start with ones like – the you who has temper tantrums, the you who sulks, the you who pouts, the you who whinges, the you who curses, the you who bullies, the you who falls into victim mode and the you who huffs and puffs, and so on.

As you can see, there are many aspects to our personality which can play out, day after day. The funny thing is we are almost always unaware of when we are in any of these roles or personalities, whilst other people often see us playing out these various roles.

Have some fun with this exercise and if you have a good friend or the freedom to do this safely with your partner, try to highlight each other's different personalities. Playing with these aspects makes them more clear, understandable and meaningful. For couples and even friends, this can be a great revelation and can help to put an end to many misunderstandings and conflicts.

I have named the one who I am always trying to stay connected with, as 'Grand Master Adrian'. When I fully engage with Grand Master Adrian I am much more centred and present – I am a more real, authentic and conscious decision maker. Sometimes, if I am being a real nong and acting from a less desirable character or personality, I am sent up to the man-shed by Arleen, to find and reconnect with Grand Master Adrian. Some other identities within me are: The Punk, Mr Uneducated, Little Alone Boy, Mr Angry and Little I cannot have it, Adrian. When we begin to observe ourselves and our behaviour we can begin to see the many roles we play, depending on the situation in which we find ourselves. Learning to recognise this and become more in charge is quite another story. It takes lots of practice, courage and skill to progress on our journey to become the master of our many personalities.

Part of the process of self-mastery is about moving on from our past and even our present situation and visualising and working towards a new paradigm, vision, dream or goal, to what I call our 'Future Potential Self'. It is one thing to work in the moment and in the now, but I believe that it is wise to have a vision, goal, dream and idea of where I am wishing to go, even if I am not 100% sure of how I will get there. Writing this book has been a great example of that. I knew that I wanted to get it written, published and out into the world, that was my goal and vision and had I not had that to hold, then writing it would have been much less of a necessity or reason. Reasons for doing things are often future based and I believe that planning and dreaming and visualising my future is just as important as living in the now, in the moment. For me the 'staying in the now' mantra becomes a bit of a head trip and I know that when I focus on what I want or wish for (in the future) I get more motivated and energised and excited about all that can become a reality.

As I said to a good friend once when we were sharing our thoughts on 'the now', I said, *"Even Eckhart Tolle would have a diary to write down his future plans and appointments!"*

For me, when I choose to move on from my Present Self, and the me that I am now, to my Future Potential Self, I get a sense of empowerment and growth as I feel my potential mounting and spilling out.

Chapter Eight

From Present Self to Future Potential Self

When working with people who want to move on in their life or from their current situation; moving from their Present Self perspective, position or situation – from where they are *Right Now* – to who they wish to be, or to what they want to achieve in the future, we work with what I call the Future Potential Self.

This is the one who knows what to wish for, the one who is clear about the path to take and the one who knows how to arrive, achieve, attain or land at this future place, at this future destination.

Gaining a sense of where we are *Right Now* is always a good place to start. Knowing where we are *Right Now* gives us a clear perspective, anchors us and gives us a solid foundation from which to work from.

To begin this exercise you will need some paper or your journal.

Collect some coloured pencils or crayons for drawing an expressive representation of how you are in this moment, *Right Now*.

Where Am 'I' Right Now?

A useful way to begin this process is to close your eyes and get a sense of how you really are *Right Now*. See, sense and feel from the inside how you are and then allow yourself, as freely as you can, without too much thinking, to choose the colours, shapes and movements to draw your Present Self on the paper. Try to be as abstract and creative as you can. The important thing is to allow the process to unfold freely, allowing your creative juices to flow…

It is a good idea to put the date on the picture (and any other work you do) as a reference point for the progress of your journey.

When you have created the picture of your Present Self, visualize the person that you would like to be in say three days, three weeks or three months' time, as a Future Potential You. Then notice 'the gap' between them both. What would be your next step to change, to let go of and to gain, in order to take that next step, from the Present You to the Future Potential You? Ask yourself this question and from here you can begin to plan, create and finally become this future you.

I have used this exercise hundreds of times with individual clients and students and with groups and every time that I do it I witness wonderful positive changes. So please, do this exercise for yourself and observe the changes you make over the following days, weeks or months.

Using the four steps outlined below will give you a clearer path and understanding of the process.

The four steps are Visioning, Creating, Planning and Acting.

1. To begin with you must 'vision' what you want and how you want to be.

2. Once you have your vision, you need to 'create' and 'dramatize' it so you can begin to sense a change is evolving. Creating the vision with drawings, sculptures, poems, writing, song, movement or any other form of creative endeavour. Dramatizing (acting and moving) will help you to feel and own it (See the following pages for more on dramatizing).

3. The next stage is 'planning' how and when you are going to do the things you have in your vision and have created. This is a crucial part of moving from where you are *Right Now* to where you wish to be. Planning takes some effort, but once it is in process you will have a road map to keep you focused and on the road.

4. The final stage is to 'act', to actually use your will and do it. It is generally quite easy to visualize, create and plan what it is we want but it is quite another thing to actually do it. The action you take will give you the results.

Physically, emotionally, mentally and spiritually we seem to have gotten everything upside down or inside out. We have too many wars instead of peace, too much starvation instead of a world of plenty and too much hatred instead of love. We smoke, eat, drink and breathe poisons and toxins that we know are dangerous for our health and wellbeing and we continue to rape and pillage the earth of is natural, diminishing resources. This is what I mean by living in a less than fully present state of being and if we do not take stock of Where we are *Right Now* and do something dramatic and real, then the future looks pretty grim. Hopefully, there will be enough energy devoted to changing our consciousness globally and collectively halt this juggernaut of destruction and mayhem.

Where Am 'I' Right Now?

It is good practice to take a moment now and then and consider our own actions and see how we might choose and manage to restore and replenish ourselves and our own lives, if they are in need of it. As we become more conscious of our own thoughts, feelings and actions, we can then begin to lead by example and hopefully help others to do the same. As we know, we cannot change other people, we can only change ourselves.

The Coaching that I do is about working from the Present Self and situation to this Future Potential. I get people to paint, draw, sculpt, move, dance, speak and act out their future potential and I get them to name him or her so that they have a fixed point to focus on and keep coming back to, or in our case move towards.

I worked with one client who had a real challenge in moving forward towards her vocational goal. She was really challenged by becoming successful and being out there. After some time spent with her working on building up the vision of her future self, we then went step by step and introduced new things each week for her to get used to. As she stepped into the role of this new identity, this new Future Potential Self, she steadily became more comfortable with it. One of the big issues that she faced was what her friends and family might think of her if she really became successful, especially financially. It is nice to be able to say that she is now well on her way to being the successful woman that she wanted to become.

One thing that we can work on to help us to actually realise our goals and dreams in life, is working with our personal and professional boundaries, especially if they are unconscious, thin, flimsy or perhaps even non-existent.

Chapter Nine

Creating Healthy Boundaries

Boundaries are always very important to highlight and talk about in personal, professional or spiritual development work. Learning how to develop, maintain and use our boundaries is, I believe, essential in all areas of our lives.

Boundaries are essential for not only my clients but for me too as a therapist and trainer. If I did not have strong personal and professional boundaries I would not be able to work very effectively, safely or efficiently. As someone choosing to take on these roles I am setting myself up for being bullied, intimated, manipulated or projected upon if I am not holding a strong and healthy boundary. People working in the field of human services often become burnt-out at some time in their career (often within the first three years) and from my observations after several years of working in this industry I would say that this is more than partly due to people not creating, understanding or using healthy boundaries.

Working alongside other people in any job or industry can be very challenging and when compounded with challenging clients, disgruntled or unpleasant colleagues and at times overpowering and demanding bosses, the task of staying centred and stress free can be very difficult. This is a good enough reason why we need to learn how to create and maintain healthy boundaries. This is very much about self-preservation!

I regularly work with people who need to develop or strengthen their boundaries in some area of their life. Without healthy and strong boundaries, they can easily become physically, emotionally, mentally or spiritually ill.

Creating a strong and healthy boundary

Firstly, by using your imagination, you can learn how to create a safe and healthy boundary. To begin this exercise, imagine a sheath, a wall, or an energy field around you. For simplicity I will refer to this as your 'energy field'. Imagine the edge or boundary to this energy field being about a metre from your physical body. A great way to help you to do this is for you to walk around and create it with your hands. Imagine that you can feel the inside of this boundary, as if it had a skin (think of a big bubble). Even though it has a skin, this energy field is see-through and invisible. Try to sense this energy bubble being around you as you walk around. Sense it all around you – front, back, sides, above and below. Make it colourful if you wish too.

As you create this energy bubble, begin to tell yourself that you are the only one allowed inside this bubble. Make a statement to yourself that 'no one else' is allowed in. After a few minutes of getting used to this space (where no one else is allowed in) imagine your whole being filling this space, physically, emotionally, mentally and spiritually. Imagine and allow your whole being to be encapsulated and surrounded and contained within this new energy bubble. Claim it as yours, as part of you – Private – No Entry!

And now to test your new boundary energy bubble.

Walk around for a while longer getting used to it some more. Now, imagine someone is walking towards you and trying to enter into your energy bubble. Imagine that your boundary stops them in their tracks, not allowing them into your energy field, your energy bubble; your space.

By creating this new boundary you will become more aware of how to use it in future situations. Be aware of how you are with your new boundary, energy field or energy bubble, *Right Now*. Practice this over and over again until you feel you have created a strong and permanent boundary.

We are not usually fully aware of our energetic boundaries, but by practicing being in our 'I' presence we can become much more aware. By practicing this exercise regularly you will become more aware of being present and feel a lot more protected, safe and centred.

One word that goes well with boundary work is the word NO. I worked with a woman recently who wrote the word NO on her hand as a reminder to say it more often and it really worked. I should know – it was my wife Arleen! While working through an issue together it became apparent that she struggled with holding her position, her boundary, and saying no in a particular area of her life. As part of her process in learning to say no, she wrote NO on her hand. With practice, it has now become a word which she can express more freely. Subsequently, we have both used the 'NO on the hand' process to support clients who are challenged with expressing this word.

Where Am 'I' Right Now?

Boundary work is a common part of my coaching, counselling and psychotherapy work. One woman that I worked with found that the words 'Not Now' were right for her as a way of staying in her power. Creating and holding boundaries is something well worth practicing, and using a simple word or statement can be fun, strengthening and supportive.

By developing our new boundaries we may well begin to experience our relationships in different ways. To begin with, people may be somewhat challenged and/or surprised by this new way in which we behave and speak. However, after a short time a new sense of respect generally begins to develop as we become clearer about our position and our needs. Learning to express ourselves fully, speak truly and feel safe in a protected boundary will change the way in which we communicate with people. Many of the anxieties, stresses, fears and doubts which we may have previously carried often diminish. If you skipped the exercise on creating a healthy boundary, this may be a good time to stop reading, go back and do it.

My personal way of checking my energy space, my boundaries, is by using a few words as a reminder that this space is my space and it is not to be invaded by anyone or anything. *"Nothing is allowed in unless it is invited"* is a powerful saying and reminder for me about staying in my power.

This next exercise is not dissimilar to the energy bubble building exercise and offers you a way of staying more present and full of energy. In this exercise you will be asked to take your energy levels up and down so that you can learn how to control and choose what energy and presence level you would like to be in at any given time.

First of all, take a moment to relax. This is always a good place to start with any personal development work – relax and breathe. Take your time. Give yourself a few minutes.

Slowing down and taking time out for ourselves to become more fully present is a powerful and fulfilling thing to do. Imagine if everyone in the whole world took just nine minutes out each day to relax and focus within and took the time to choose to be more conscious of their thoughts, feelings and actions. Wow – what a world it would be!

You will need to stand up to do this next exercise

The first step in the exercise is to pump your energy level up. So, go on, stand up and stamp on the ground, wave your arms in the air, puff out your chest, stand tall, flex your muscles, loosen your neck and shoulders and breathe deeply. Spend about a minute doing this until you feel much more energized.

Pumping up our energy is something we don't often do unless we go to the gym or partake in a practice of yoga, martial arts, a sport or an exercise routine of some kind. So, pump away and get that energy moving.

Now that you are all pumped up, the next step is to allow (perhaps even force) yourself to feel a bit less energized than you are *Right Now*. Use your imagination and body to take your energy level down about five or ten percent and allow your arms, legs and back to feel weaker. Keep taking your energy level down in five or ten percent increments until you reach what you think and feel is your normal everyday operating energy level.

If you are a high energy, go getter type of person who is very fit, active and motivated, you will only need to go down a few notches from your highly pumped energy level to reach your general everyday level. I measure my average everyday energetic operating level at about eighty – eighty five percent as I am quite a high energy and motivated person and when I am doing this exercise I pump my energy up to as close as one hundred percent as possible and bring it down in five percent increments to reach and feel my everyday eighty – eighty five percent operating level.

Getting to know this place is one thing, getting to know the other places that we visit, both above and below this general place of living our lives is also beneficial.

To get to know the bottom end of the spectrum, keep taking your energy level down until you are on the floor or in a bent over position. Feel what it is like to be flat. Stay there for a moment and really feel it. We all go there on occasions; some more than others. Once we get to know this place too and feel what it is like to be there, we can make a choice to move out of it. In this place we can ask the question, Where Am 'I' *Right Now*? and then make a choice to move out of it and be in a better place!

Notice how you feel in this low energy place and then slowly bring yourself up again in small five – ten percent increments until you again reach your chosen place of balance. Once you have reached this place take a moment to sense what it might be like to live and operate from this energy level every day. Imagine what else you could you get done with this new energy. What goals and dreams could you strive towards and reach with this new energy? Obviously living and operating at one hundred percent is not always possible, but being at seventy – eighty percent is very possible and is actually quite a high level.

Once you are in this space, get to know it. Lock it into your memory hard-drive. This is the place to get to know and this is the place where you can consciously choose to be (at minimum) every day if you wish to. From this place you will be much more able to set, tackle and achieve just about anything that you wish for.

This expansion and contraction of energy can also be demonstrated using a balloon. Blowing up a balloon to represent where we are *Right Now* and then inflating and deflating it to represent your different energy levels, from low to high will give you a good visual of what is happening. It is also a lot of fun.

So yes, you have guessed it – go and get yourself a balloon and have some fun!

Choosing to operate at a higher energy level or frequency is something we can all choose to do. Choosing to put it into action is often the challenge. Looking at and changing some of our habits, thoughts, actions, beliefs and behaviours are essential if we are wanting to operate and live from this higher level energy place. Our diet, exercise, recreation, relationships and general lifestyles may have to change, perhaps even dramatically, if we are serious about transformation and growth.

Taking the time and energy to put all of this in place usually takes some serious planning to begin with. If you wish to step into a new, higher level of energy, what is it you have to do to make it happen? Take your journal and begin making notes and plans *Right Now* and start your own decision making process of what you need to do.

As we now know, healthy boundaries are essential if we are to take our journey of personal and spiritual work seriously. When working with men I often work with them on creating and working with boundaries as well as with anger, vocation, communication and other topics. I call this work 'Empowering Men'.

Chapter Ten

Empowering Men

Over the past fifteen plus years I have been creating and facilitating workshops, journeys into the bush and sacred circles as a way of supporting men to learn how to become more aware, more conscious and more responsible for their behaviour and their lives. The men who choose to step in and make a commitment to doing this powerful and life changing work learn how to change the way in which they communicate, think, feel and act in the world and become better men.

I have had the honour and the privilege to experience very deep and profound shifts in hundreds of men's lives and feel a deep sense of gratitude to all of the men who have put their trust in sharing this work with me. Many men in our western culture feel unsafe in the presence of other strong, powerful, switched on and emotionally intelligent men and the thought of sharing an emotional space for many men – is just too much of a challenge. However, I find that with almost all men, once they have built up the courage to attend a Men's Circle or a Men's Workshop, they love it.

As with all personal development work, there are many challenges to work through in men's work too and sometimes there are walls or blocks to encounter along the way. Some men seem to soldier along, working through their 'stuff' really well and then suddenly – bang – they are gone; disappearing back into the proverbial cave never to be seen or heard from again.

Where Am 'I' Right Now?

A good friend of mine, Jeremiah, says that attending Men's Groups is not only a gift to him, but a gift to his family, as he grows and develops himself. Men, like Jeremiah, who attend Men's Groups for a long period of time, really help to hold the space for other men to feel safe, comfortable and heard, especially for new men. Men like this are a great inspiration to other men. When I hear the depth of the sharing and communication between men each week I am saddened that more men do not step up and challenge themselves to engage with deeper, emotional, psychotherapeutic work, as it can make a huge difference to their life, their partners and their children. What a difference it makes to have good strong, confident and mature men in the community.

Generally, men have not had the greatest of role models and it is, I believe, time to change this. For the men reading this book – Where are you, *Right Now* with your sense of being a good man in the community. Can you honestly say that you are standing tall?

I would like to encourage and challenge you to seek out a Men's Group or Men's Social Group which supports, encourages and challenges you to go deeper in your exploration of being a better man. There are now thousands of Men's Groups and Men's Organisations in the world and each week I hear of new ones forming. Locally, in Australia, we have several great Men's Organisations. One such organisation is 'Men's Wellbeing' which has a membership of several hundred men. They offer workshops and training and very special men's gatherings over three or four days where up to one hundred and fifty men meet up and share time and energy together in conversation, workshops and socializing. I highly recommend all men get involved with an organisation or Men's Group to support them on their journey.

We also have the pleasure of having Steve Biddulph here in

Australia. He helped to revolutionise the Men's Movement back in the nineties with his book *Manhood*. He has sold over a million and a half copies world-wide.

White Ribbon is an organisation that does some wonderful work and I have become an Ambassador for them to support the work that they do. Their work is focused on bringing awareness to Domestic Violence and working to stop it. Closely linked to this work is The CEO Challenge in Brisbane that I have also connected with and support. One of the highlights of the CEO Challenge is an annual run called The Darkness to Daylight Challenge, where people run through the night covering distances of up to 110 kilometres; which represents the amount of people killed on average in Australia each year through Domestic Violence.

This is a huge issue not just in Australia but every country in the world and the more that we work together the more we can bring this issue to people's attention and at least try and stop it from growing and even hopefully begin to reverse the statistics. In the men's work that I do, looking at anger, rage and domestic violence is a touchy and sensitive, yet very important issue to work with. Knowing how to work with this topic with the right balance of sensitivity and directness is important as there is often a sense of guilt and shame that goes with it for many men.

Owning our anger

Many, if not all men carry some degree of anger. Some have learned to bottle it up and keep it suppressed whilst other men just let it out uncontrollably and sometimes dangerously. Neither of these has really proven to be a skilful way in which to deal with it. Learning to own and deal with our anger is a very empowering and worthy thing to do.

Working with anger can be a challenging and deeply emotional process. I always feel moved when men come to a place of owning and controlling their anger, especially with men who are in a relationship with a woman. This work can be profound as it can positively change the relationship between a man and a woman if the man can really take on the process, gain insights and make some new changes. Working with anger exercises can bring a deep awareness to men of how they may be communicating with their partner, wife or lover; when they are not fully present and when their anger is present.

Here is an example of the anger management process that I have developed:

Six men stood in a circle imagining that their feet were super-glued to the floor and that their partner, wife, or lover, was standing in front of them. The men were asked to remember a time when they were angry or in a raging mood with this person.

After a few moments, the men indicate that they have an image of their 'woman' to work with. I then ask them to pump up their anger, as I count down from ten to one – ten, nine, eight, seven, six …*"build it up, feel the anger. Feel the rage"* … five, four … *"when I get to one, let her have it"*… three, two, one. On the count of one, the men yell, holler or scream out their anger and rage at the imaginary person before them…The room goes still, quiet and we wait. We wait for about twenty seconds. The mood in the room is palpable. Holding the raw energy, I speak softly and gently and ask the men to acknowledge where they are *Right Now* and to allow their feelings to be real. I ask them to be in touch with what they are feeling and be with it for a few moments.

I ask: "What must it be like for your woman? What must it be like for her to be on the receiving end of that anger or rage?"

I point out that it is nearly always the woman who is in the position of being physically inferior to men.

"What would it be like, for her? What would it be like to be in her shoes?"

I allow the men to stay in their quiet space for a while longer before asking each man to describe what is going on for him. I ask each man to say a word or a short sentence to convey how they are feeling.

This is where emotions really start to flow. As the penny drops, the men become very emotional. The powerful strength of self-realization in this moment for many men is not lost. This is where the realization hits them about how they can overpower and appear dangerous and unsafe to their partners – to females, to women, and perhaps even to their children, friends, family members or their male partners if they are in a same sex relationship.

Owning this aspect of our being can be very challenging. On one level, it can be very frightening to face one's anger, and yet, on another level, it can be very empowering. As men, it can give us a real sense of how we can learn to control our rage and anger. We can learn to channel this powerful energy in new and less aggressive and destructive ways by knowing and understanding it. To be able to own and work and transform this enormously potent and powerfully destructive element of our being is very empowering.

Men's work is powerful and oftentimes challenging and I am proud to be part of a wide network of men in the world who have the courage to step in and work with it. I am aware of the possibility of reactions, projections, judgments and thoughts and feelings that men can have towards a facilitator and it does take quite a lot of courage to do this work every week. I would like to honour all the men who have the courage and will to do this work in the world. *"Thank you Good Men!"*

Working with anger is one of the many things that I get to work with in terms of personal and spiritual development. From my experience of working with my own, and with literally 1000's of other people's emotions and soul processes over the past twenty years, I hold the opinion that anger is a symptom of something being out of place, out of balance; things such as love, contentment, joy, satisfaction, clarity or even courage.

When we start to investigate and understand ourselves from a deeper, more soulful perspective we will begin to observe and see that there are a several aspects of our being that other, sub-natures or sub-behaviours stem from, just as anger tends to do.

The three major aspects that I work with are fear, doubt and (self) hatred.

Chapter Eleven

Fear, Doubt and (Self) Hatred

I have come to a firm belief that one of the greatest challenges that we have, in terms of becoming masters of our own lives, is to wrestle with and overcome the power, influence and energy of 'fear', 'doubt' and (self) 'hatred'.

Rudolf Steiner named these three powerful beings or energies, The Three Beasts.

When working with these issues, artistic and dramatic expression can help to show us the reality of how these Three Beasts live within and around us. Each of them has a particular energy and it becomes possible after some serious study, to develop an image and understanding of what they look like and how they operate. With this knowledge and understanding we can learn how to be more conscious and more present in our 'I'. By disclosing and naming these Three Beasts, they lose their power. If you have read or watched the Harry Potter stories, you will remember how Harry would always speak the name "*Voltemort*", while others would not. This helped Harry to diminish and shrink Voltemort's power over him and help him to overcome his fear by growing his courage.

Each of these Three Beasts has a counterpart, an antidote or a remedy, which we can find within and use to help us to be more in our 'I' presence.

Doubt, hatred and fear are intrinsically linked to the head (as doubt in thinking), heart (as feeling hatred), and limbs (as fear of taking action/willing). Thinking, Feeling and Willing will be explored further in the next chapter.

The following is an outline of how these counterparts, antidotes or remedies can be used to overcome and control fear, doubt and (self) hatred.

When we are in 'thinking' mode we connect with our 'nervous system' and to our 'imagination'. If we are not clear and in our thinking and cognitive powers then the element of 'doubt' can creep in and take over. 'Clarity' of thinking, creative imaginative thinking and self-belief are remedies to develop for overcoming doubt.

When we are in 'feeling' mode we connect with our 'rhythmical system' and to our 'inspiration'. If we are in any form of 'hatred' or dislike, then 'love' and compassion, are remedies we can develop to overcome them.

When we are in action and using our 'will' (doing) forces, we connect with our 'metabolic system' and our 'intuition'. If we wish to overcome 'fear', then the act of 'courage' is our remedy.

It takes much inner spiritual work to really overcome or transform these three beasts. The tools of creative imagination and expression through art, movement and drama are very good ways to help us work with and through the process of fear, doubt and (self) hatred.

Personal and spiritual development is very much about changing the way in which we feel about ourselves and learning to fully love ourselves. This is possibly the most empowering thing we can do; to love ourselves wholeheartedly.

Doubt is something that can diminish us to feeling unworthy

and confused and can often lead to procrastination, which keeps us stuck in our lives. Fear can grip us in panic, anxiety, stagnation or even terror. Self-love, self-belief and courage are the cornerstones of being fully in 'I' presence.

Take some time *Right Now* to consider where you are in self-love, self-belief and courage. Take some time to name and own what you have to face in your life and see where and what you have to do to face these things. This exercise will keep you very busy. Facing these challenges will be a challenge in itself.

I know for myself that I have had to face many things in my life that were huge tasks or challenges. At the time of having to face them, I often felt as if I had walked into an avalanche. At these times my fears and doubts were often huge and my self-love and self-esteem were often very small. It took me lots of soul searching and self-talk to work my way through these situations. With the knowledge of how to engage the tools of imagination, inspiration and intuition I was much more able to work through these challenges. Some of the greatest gifts and learning can come during times of panic, procrastination, confusion and terror where our sense of self and 'I' presence is challenged to overcome our fear, doubt and self-hatred.

The Meeting

Several years ago, while on a small Scottish island, I was faced with meeting a new spirit guide. As I was climbing up a mountain in search of finding an answer to a question that was sitting deep within me, I thought that perhaps I had lost all my senses and had gone totally mad as I met and then conversed with this spiritual being who stood before me.

Adrian's Scottish story

In 2003 I made a decision to leave my marriage of sixteen years. I was on a soul searching mission to 'find myself' and was visiting a small Scottish isle on the west-coast of Scotland called Eigg, near the well-known Isle of Skye. I had decided to visit this island after having a profound dream/memory of a past life on the island sometime between the tenth and fourteenth century. This dream (and memory) was intensified when a friend, who was in the dream with me, came to visit me two weeks later and told me that she had just re-composed a song that had been written on the Isle of Eigg a hundred or so years ago – very spooky!

Walking alone, up the side of the steep 393 metre mountain, called An Sgurr, the only large outcrop of any description on the isle, I was in a meditative mood, trying hard to decide where and what I would do next in my life. I had just been to South Africa for a few weeks and was due to fly to Sri Lanka for a month, a lifelong dream that seemed so close to becoming a reality. There was something troubling me; I was not sure if I should return to South Africa instead of going on to Sri Lanka.

I was about three quarters of the way to the top of the mountain and just about to step between two massive boulders to continue my way on the trail, when I 'saw' him. He was standing right in front of me. My spiritual study, training and experiences had given me connections with spiritual beings previously so at least I was somewhat prepared for what was happening; however this being

Fear, Doubt and (Self) Hatred

was big and somewhat intimidating and scary. He appeared to me as a Viking type character and stood towering in front of me. Yes, I know sometimes that these stories seem far-fetched – but bear with me … it was what I experienced.

I felt that this spirit being was a spirit guardian of sorts, perhaps, a guardian of the mountain. I began to communicate with him and asked for permission to continue, to walk to the top of the mountain. He gave me the permission that I sought by stepping aside. Waking past him and through the two boulders certainly felt as if I had stepped through a portal of sorts. This Viking character has been with me as a guide ever since.

I walked on to the top of An Sgurr as if meeting a spiritual being was a normal everyday thing to do and spent a couple of hours in deep meditation searching for an answer to my question and dilemma; should I return to South Africa or go on to Sri Lanka? I felt deep within my soul that this decision would be one of the most profound and important decisions that I would ever make. I cannot explain how I knew this – I just knew.

As I sat on top of An Sgurr I decided that I would strip off and sit naked in meditation to fully expose myself to the elements.

And this is the funny bit. As I sat in meditation, butt naked on top of the mountain, my meditation was abruptly and noisily interrupted by a loud booming noise. As I opened my eyes to see what this intrusion to my meditation was, I saw, what I think was an F1-11 fighter jet, or something like one, zooming past me only about two hundred and fifty metres away from where I sat. It zoomed on past me and then, much to my surprise, it reappeared several seconds later, this time even a little bit closer. As the jet fighter was passing me for the second time I got eye to eye contact with the pilot! I can only image his surprise at seeing me butt naked on the mountain top and the story he had for his mates when he got back to the Royal Air Force base.

One week later I went to Amsterdam in Holland and into the KLM airline office and exchanged, free of charge, my one-way round the world ticket and went back to South Africa. Of course that is where I decided to begin a new life with Arleen, which happened when we started our relationship about a year later. It was, during this time, where I really had to dig deep and face many of my own fears, doubts and self-hatred. It was during this time in South Africa that I really came of age and stepped into my deeper, more mature manhood as well as my 'I' presence (are they the same?) more fully than I had ever done before in my life. I challenged myself to go through several initiations of sorts and am so glad that I did so, as I now see the results.

And just to complete the story; for my fiftieth birthday I had a tattoo put on my arm. The tattoo was created intuitively by the tattoo artist Josh from only a small amount of input from me. The resemblance to the Viking sketch that I did about a week after our meeting on the mountainside is amazing!

I have a team of spirit guides who I regularly connect and work with, one of which is my old mate The Viking from An Scurr. He brings me much knowledge and wisdom and strength and I love his presence.

The following poem by Marianne Williamson typifies, for me, what my life journey is all about. It really has been a journey of allowing the light to shine through and accepting my special gifts and talents. As Marianne Williamson clearly highlights in her poem, we really are born to shine, even though we often find it a challenge to do so.

This poem is often found on the internet, incorrectly accredited to Nelson Mandela, linking it to his inauguration speech in 1994, and especially because of the last sentence of the poem: *"As we are liberated from our own fear, our presence automatically liberates others."* He did not actually use these words. He said: *"We have, at last, achieved our political emancipation. We pledge ourselves to liberate all our people from the continuing bondage of poverty, deprivation, suffering, gender and other discrimination".*

By Marianne Williamson

Our deepest fear is not that we are inadequate.

Our deepest fear is that we are powerful beyond measure

It is our light, not our darkness that most frightens us

We ask ourselves, who am I to be brilliant

gorgeous, talented, fabulous?

Actually, who are you not to be? You are a child of God.

Your playing small does not serve the world

There is nothing enlightened about shrinking

so that other people won't feel insecure around you

We are all meant to shine, as children do

We were born to make manifest the glory of God that is within us

It's not just in some of us; it's in everyone.

And as we let our own light shine

Where Am 'I' Right Now?

we unconsciously give other people

permission to do the same.

As we are liberated from our own fear,

our presence automatically liberates others.

One of the highlights in my life, that I love to recall from time to time, occurred in 2004 on a visit to Robben Island. Here, on this island, I played my didgeridoo through the doorway of Nelson Mandela's old cell. Sharing this experience with me were a few friends and two Robben Island tour guides, both ex inmates themselves. The small cell is only about three metres by three metres. Mandela spent eighteen years of his full twenty eight year incarceration in this cell, with only the very basic of items. Playing my didgeridoo there was a spine chilling and emotional experience and one that brings Nelson Mandela (Madiba) to mind when I remember it. He is one of the people who inspire me the most. I do not know all of what occurred to set him free or what might have happened behind closed doors, but I do know that for anyone who had to endure those years in prison and then come out and think, feel, speak and act in the manner that he did, is a person to fully respect and admire. He certainly made some very empowering decisions in his life.

When making any decision it is always a good idea to do it from a very conscious place. One way to do this is to bring in our thinking, our feeling and our will so that we have a more balanced view, understanding and perspective.

Chapter Twelve

Thinking, Feeling and Willing

Thinking, feeling and willing (doing or acting) are aspects of our 'I' which are instrumental in determining how we live our lives. Observing and understanding these three aspects of our being are important if we truly wish to understand how we think, feel and act or operate in the world.

When working through a difficult situation or challenge in our life it is useful to have an understanding of these three aspects as they generally carry answers to our challenges or issues. Our challenges and issues are almost always connected to our thinking, our feelings or our actions, or lack thereof.

When the topic of thinking, feeling and willing is introduced into my workshops, I ask everyone to do a little dance so that they can connect with these three aspects in a fun and entertaining way.

Why not try it for yourself. Come on, stand up. Yes, go on, up you get, don't be shy!

Where Am 'I' Right Now?

The dance goes like this:

Walk around the space you are in and tap yourself on your forehead with the palm of your hand – one – two – three – times. Then tap on your chest, near your heart – one – two – three times. Keep walking around. Next, click your fingers – one – two – three – times. And then back to the beginning and back to your forehead again. Tapping – one – two – three. Then on your chest again – one – two – three and then click your fingers – one – two – three. Keep this going until you get a steady rhythm and a sense that you are doing this in a state of balance in your thinking, feeling and willing. Being in a state of clear consciousness can be helpful in how we live our lives and this little exercise can act as a good reminder of how to stay present and focused.

> **Head (forehead) – tap, tap, tap; Heart (chest) – tap, tap, tap; Limbs (fingers) – click, click, click.**

Whenever we have a problem or a challenge, we can work towards creating a sense of balance in our thinking, feeling and willing. For instance, my old habit and tendency of rushing into things with a strong force of will has occasionally led to less than ideal outcomes or results. Using this exercise has made a lot of difference in how I go about my daily business.

Take some time now to reflect on how you operate in the world. Are you generally more predominant in thinking, feeling or willing? When you have an understanding of this, try finding ways to bring in the other less dominant aspects and work towards creating a sense of balancing or alignment of all three.

For anyone with a habit of being intoxicated with alcohol, nicotine or any other drug that plays havoc with the senses, it is more difficult to create a balance in thinking, feeling and willing, as these substances dull our ability to think clearly, or to feel and act in a clear and conscious way. It is by working with clarity in forming our thoughts, engaging with the depth and pulse of our feelings and using our courage and strength in our actions, that helps us to truly overcome our fears and doubts, as well as our reactions, projections and judgements.

Choose to spend some time with this and you will experience some amazing results. If you choose to work on mastering this, and other aspects of your being, you will be well on the way to improving your conscious awareness and life in a whole new way.

Each day spent doing these exercises will bring fresh insights and wisdom and is certainly worth the time, energy and effort required. As you get deeper and deeper down the rabbit hole of self-investigation and self-awareness you will begin to notice and observe more and more how you relate to and communicate with people. One powerful thing that I love to work with is understanding how I react, project and judge people. This is a very powerful, but often challenging topic to work with, as it can stir up some deep emotions and feelings.

Chapter Thirteen

Reactions, Projections and Judgements

Our reactions, projections and judgements are mostly driven and expressed from our unconscious. Once they have been released and expressed, we often dislike or regret them. Being part of our soul make-up, it generally requires a good amount of focus and effort to fully observe how these actually come alive and work within and through us.

For more clarity, I would first like to outline what I mean by reactions, projections and judgements from a therapeutic and human development perspective.

As we travel through life and meet people or situations we 'respond' naturally with what we call 'fight or flight' if we are not comfortable in the situation. We also spend much of our time in a place of reaction, projection or judgement with people when we are not in a place of safety, trust and conscious awareness and are not standing in our 'I' presence. When we meet people, especially for the first time, we often link them to persons or situations from our own past; from our past experiences, beliefs, assumptions or values. So let us agree that these soul activities (reactions, projections and judgements) do not represent the best of us and let's agree that the way in which they are used and expressed in this book is from a negative or non-serving perspective.

In the case of judgement, it can be good to make a judgement if it is to make a decision about something or someone that has a positive outcome. Judging from a place of discernment and intuition about something or someone can be a good thing, especially if we need to create a boundary or protection. However, a judgement about how someone should live their life, walk their dog, look or speak is another matter. There is a big difference in being discerning or making an intuitive or informative decision about something or someone and making a call on someone's behaviour, action or character.

This is the distinction that I would like to make here so that we are clear on the use of the word judgement. Judgement then, in terms of what this book is covering is: a judgement of someone's character, behaviour or action that comes from a place that is not discerning, intuitive or informative, but one that has probably stemmed from a reaction or projection of some kind, most likely from something that has happened in the past.

Judgements, reactions and projections are often jumbled up and intertwined and it is not always easy to decipher which one is operating at any given time. When one or more of these is brought to our awareness we can start to see and experience how our behaviour or actions can affect people. At first, this awakening and awareness to how we behave can be quite a shock. When we are in a place of reaction, projection or judgement, it generally means that our 'I' presence has diminished.

Learning not to react, project and judge others is not an easy task. Unless we have done a fair amount of work on ourselves in this area and have learnt how to overcome and control these thoughts, feelings and behaviours, we will almost certainly go into nano-second judgement, reaction or projection mode when we meet someone or are placed in a new situation. Our judgements can leap up and create stories so quickly that they are difficult to observe, catch and stop. Stories such as – he is too fat, she is too well dressed, he is not very smart, they are all too rich or too poor, or too happy – can go through our minds in nano-seconds and before we know it, we have made a judgement. From here we often go into reaction. We are sometimes so quick to react, judge or project that we can get the wrong message, miss the point or totally misinterpret the situation and from here we can then easily get ourselves into a sticky or uncomfortable situation.

The following story is a lovely way to express this.

A fifty five year old man popped into the super market to buy a bag of sugar and a box of tea bags during his morning tea break and was in a bit of a hurry. When he arrived at the checkout there was a woman with a baby in her arms talking to the cashier. He could feel his impatience growing. He started to fret and tap his feet and after about three minutes he leant forward and in quite a rude manner, said *"Can you hurry up – I have only popped in for two items and you are holding up the queue!"*

The woman with the baby in her arms looked upset and walked out of the shop. The man turned to the young cashier and said, *"Ah, some people just make life so difficult. The checkout is not a place to stop and have idle chats"*.

The young cashier looked up at the man with a tear in her eye. *"That is my baby sir"*, she said. *"The only time I get to see him during the day is when my sister brings him in to see me in the morning and in the afternoon for a few minutes. I am a single mum and have to work as much as I can to pay for me and my baby"*.

The man had misjudged the situation, reacted and jumped quickly to conclusions. How many times are we guilty of doing something similar ourselves? Our impatience, selfishness, fears and doubts and our lack of concern and love for other people help to feed our judgements and reactions. Choosing and learning to switch these behaviours off will take a certain amount of commitment but it is well worth doing.

Once we become more centred and in our 'I' presence and become more aware of our thoughts, feelings and actions, reactions, projections and judgements, fears, doubts and lack of self-love, we can then connect to other people and situations in a way that is more real and authentic. As long as we continue to make judgements and react and project our thoughts and feelings out to the world, we will stay stuck.

One good way to start working with this is to spend a moment or two before each new meeting or situation, asking yourself the question – Where Am 'I' *Right Now?* Every time you do this and ask this question you will have a choice to bring yourself back to being more centred. If you are feeling agitated, nervous, scared, intimidated, angry, upset, victimized, overpowered or silly, you can turn this around by giving attention to what's happening for you in the moment. This exercise is best done over a period of a week. It is based on one of my many sayings – "*Spirituality is the next person you meet.*"

What this statement is saying is; depending on whether you choose to respond and take responsibility and use your intuition or choose to use projections, reactions and judgements, will be a good measure of where you are with your spiritual development.

Once again, this is not about judging, measuring or putting people into categories. This is a self-evaluation to give you an indication of what study and work may be needed to take you to the next step of your journey of becoming more conscious.

<u>Where Am 'I' Right Now?</u>

When faced with a situation or meeting in which I am not fully comfortable I use this process and quickly remind myself of being Grand Master Adrian. One of my big challenges was singing with, and in front of other people, so to help me overcome this fear I chose to join a weekly singing group with my good friends David and Suzanne. For many years before this (and for a good time during the singing classes), I would clam up and freeze when it was my turn to sing. With lots of good safe tuition and encouragement along with the process of bringing myself into my 'I' presence, I was able to hold my own.

Soon after the third set of weekly singing courses that I attended, over an eight month period, this was put to the test at David's birthday gathering. I have attended many of his birthday gatherings over the years and know that there is always group singing, as this is what he loves to do on his birthday. As we sat around the bonfire singing, I was feeling quite confident singing along with everyone else, but then one of the songs we had learnt in the singing classes started. It was a call and response song. Although it was one of my favourites and one that I knew well, I now felt the fear rising. As we went around the circle taking the role of being the caller, the old inner voice started up – *"You are going to forget the words"* it said. Forgetting the words was always at the bottom of my singing fear. I challenged myself to tune into Mega-Star Adrian and when it was my turn to lead the call and response I pulled it off beautifully. I used my faithful process of asking myself *"Where are you Right Now Mega-Star Adrian?"* and it paid off. I am now overcoming this fear and can now sing quite confidently in a small group. Perhaps the next step of my singing challenge is to join a choir!

Having worked consciously with projections, reactions and judgements, thinking, feeling and willing and my fears, doubts and self-hatred over the past twenty or more years I am now much more able to stop the unconscious-self-talk from taking over. Of course I still find myself caught up in it all, but with each person I meet and in each situation in which I find myself – I feel more present in my 'I' and get to 'see' the person or the situation much faster and more clearly.

Having these tools in our tool bags is useful and it is a wonderful tool for therapists, facilitators and trainers as well as being very handy to use in our more intimate relationships. In my case, I am fortunate to have access to the same tools as my wife Arleen, as we both trained in Psychophonetics Counselling. Each Psychophonetics practitioner brings their own flavour to the work and my own interest and flavour has been about exploring, discovering, investigating and engaging with the 'I'. The essence of all my work is now supporting people to be more fully engaged with their 'I' presence.

A large part of my Psychophonetics and teacher training was doing drama. I loved this aspect of the training and realised, whilst doing it, that drama plays such a huge part of our lives. Come on, who is not without some sort of drama in their lives!

One way to further explore, discover and understand what we are studying, learning and choosing to engage with and adopt in our lives is to dramatize it all.

Chapter Fourteen

Dramatizing

One great way to get a get a deeper sense and understanding of how we are and what is going for us, is to dramatise the experience – to Gesture our experience and show it through a process of movement, action and sound.

The following psychotherapeutic process comes from Psychophonetics and is a useful and effective technique that I often use with clients. It is called Enter-Exit-Behold[8].

Along with the three main steps of this process (Enter, Exit and Behold), several other complimentary or additions steps can also be used, depending on the client's needs.

Here is an example of the Enter-Exit-Behold process from a personal session with a client:

This client wanted to stand more fully in his power, with promoting and working with his new vocational path of personal development leadership.

In Psychophonetics counselling we nearly always start the sessions by establishing, what we call, a Common Picture and The Wish with our clients.

To begin the session, the client, Jim (not his real name) and I spent some time in conversation to develop a Common Picture[9] and The

---

8   Enter-Exit-Behold is a Psychophonetics term.

9   Common Picture is a Psychophonetics term meaning the point when there is a

Wish[10]. We then moved into another, more specialized aspect of the Psychophonetics process, which is to work with our clients in what is best described as a 'soul awareness' process of working together to explore, discover and understand what is going on (for the client). Jim's wish was to step more deeply into his power so that he could do an evening presentation of his new personal development work, in a clear, focused and authentic way. He wanted to stay in his power and not succumb to 'selling himself short' or feeling that he was not present. He wanted to deliver his new vocational work to the public and feel really good about it.

After some further discussion, I asked Jim to imagine and show me what his old self, the one that generally shrinks or succumbs to selling himself short, looked like. I asked him to Gesture[11] firstly with his hands, and then his whole body, how this old aspect of him is experiencing this. So Jim stepped in (Step One – Enter), moved into position and gestured his experience of his 'old self'. To support clients with entering this body awareness process more easily, I sometimes say to them, *"If I were a Zulu and did not speak your language, show me with your hands and your body how you are feeling Right Now; put your words into an action and just pretend that I do not speak your language"*. I find that by making the process easier to understand it helps clients to feel less intimidated and makes this psycho-drama work more real for them.

I asked Jim to intensify the gesture, feelings and sensations for a moment – which he did – and after a few seconds, I asked him to

---

    common understanding or essence of the dynamics of client's presenting issue.

10 Wish has a specific meaning in Psychophonetics - based on the common picture, the client is invited to form a *wish*, in their own language which acts like a guide, purpose, direction or goal for the action phase part of the session.

11 Gesturing – as the *kinaesthetic mode of knowing* – is the expression of experience through bodily gestures and movement. In Psychophonetics, it has been found that every human experience can be expressed directly by most people and be understood.

step out and shake it off – to shake off the experience. Shaking off the experience of the old energy, the old self, is required so that the client can step back into their present-self and not stay stuck in the Enter experience. We have tools and processes in Psychophonetics to support people in 'getting out', if they are unable, at first, to shake off or move out of any experience that arises during a session. This is another good reason to only do this type of psychotherapeutic work with an experienced and professional practitioner. There are times when clients do get stuck or overwhelmed and knowing what to do in these circumstances is essential, both for the wellbeing and safety of the client and the health, wellbeing, protection and integrity of practitioners. As therapists, we are mindful that we are dealing with very real life situations which may have been with people for many years. It often takes clients a lot of courage and trust to open up to a practitioner and this needs to be honoured and respected.

Once out of the gesture and once the energy of the old self has been shaken off (Step two – Exit), I check to see if Jim is present. After confirming that he is present in the room and not 'stuck' in the gesture of the old self, I ask him to look back (Step three – Behold) at the Energy Imprint[12] that he had just formed in the space. This is the moment where people get to see themselves in their old make-up, in their old way of being in their world. Jim saw himself in the imprint that he had created. This moment is very real for the client and I am always careful where I step and walk, as clients really do experience these imprints as being real, as I do too. Jim went on to describe what he could 'see'. He told me he could 'see' himself as a young boy of about twelve years old. We entered into some discussion about what the boy was doing and this revealed a boy who had been 'put down' and scared to speak.

---

12 In Psychophonetics, an energy imprint may also be called an 'etheric imprint'.

Jim named this old-self. All clients who do this use the names and images that they create as anchor points. Naming these aspects of ourselves in this way help the characters we discover, to either shrink or grow, depending on our focus and needs.

Jim and I continued the process to find a place of safety for the boy, with Jim stepping in to advocate, take charge and protect the boy in certain situations, like public speaking. Jim then found a name for his new found self. With this new power-name, something like Hercules, he could stand up and protect the aptly named Little Jim.

The third step of the process is Beholding, when the client uses their imagination, insight and focus to see and observe the image that they have created from their Gesturing. Clients are often very surprised to sense or see that an energy imprint remains behind in the place that they were just in. Learning to be mindful by walking and stepping around these energy imprints in the room, becomes second nature. Using our imaginative powers, we can all learn to create and 'see' these imprints of our experiences and can learn to observe them to know what is going on. When we are 'in' the scenario, we are 'in' and when we learn to get 'out', we can look back 'in' and see it all from a totally new, more conscious and clear perspective. When we see things from this more objective perspective – which is what we do when we are 'out' and not 'in' the situation, we can make more informed and conscious choices and decisions. From this more informed and empowered position, we can choose to change and do things differently. I am glad to say that Jim's public presentation went well and he did not sell himself short.

In my work I often observe 'It', 'They', 'Him' or 'Her' as the one who people blame, accuse or identify with. When people use these terms it is generally because they are feeling victimised, and are in reaction, projection, judgement or blame mode. By using this Enter-Exit-Behold process, clients can become clearer about their current situation and can then make conscious new choices. For instance: if a person realizes, through this process, that their inner child needs some attention, they can learn to know exactly what their inner child needs because they have been able to see and understood it directly for themselves by dramatizing and by Entering in, Exiting out and Beholding exactly what their inner child was experiencing and needing. Once this knowledge is known and understood the person can then step in and give whatever is required for the inner child.

Clients are often surprised by what they observe and this can be enough to give them the courage or determination to change their behaviour and/or situation. Doing this process and gaining new observations, experiences and insights give clients a much better understanding of what is going on for them in any given moment.

I often use this process myself to deal with my own unconscious and sometimes irrational and unproductive behaviours. I like to see things from a more conscious and objective perspective and with this process I certainly can do that. It is, by far, one of the most profound and powerful psychotherapeutic processes or tools that I have come across in my twenty plus years of personal development work. It really does allow us to more fully access, understand and transform our unconscious and sometimes hidden and reactive behaviours. Arleen has seen and experienced many aspects of my behaviour over the years and we share much humour in discussing some of them, especially from a Psychophonetics counselling perspective. Arleen often takes on the role of therapist, with me as the client and I actually love the way in which she 'traps and coerces me' into seeing things from another, generally, healthier, more open and less defensive perspective, even if it does not seem that way whilst I am in a session with her. While I am in my stuff, I am not usually seeing things as clearly as I probably could be, and then – hey presto – when I am out, the world seems like a whole new and different place. Quite amazing that!

By using the Enter Exit and Behold process and many of the other Psychophonetics and Where Am 'I' *Right Now?* techniques, we can learn to illuminate and change many potentially unhealthy or unnecessary situations occurring in our lives. By attending to our daily business in a more conscious way we can dramatically reduce creating situations and reacting to people in our daily lives which do not really serve us.

Another aspect of the Psychophonetics work is using sound to support the change process in the client's experience. When working with people therapeutically and introducing sounds, I rarely ever give a particular sound for them to work with. The sounds used by clients in Psychophonetic sessions are carefully and consciously created by the practitioner and the client working together to find the sounds that are the most beneficial. The client is always the one who has the final say about which sounds best match their experience. Sounds mean different things to different people and it is good to be cautious and mindful of how we use them, especially in a therapeutic or healing setting.

In Psychophonetics, we use sounds to help enhance and clarify the client's experiences and feelings and more importantly, the effect of the sound vibrations can actually change the old inner patterns or imprints. We work as a team and we coach our clients to find the right sound to match their experience. I believe that it is almost always pointless to offer my own interpretation or opinion on what sound is to be used if it does not sit true for the client. This is a good time to leave our ego out of the equation.

Once we have found the right sound and the client has practiced it well enough, there are a number of options open to us depending on the client's circumstance and needs. These may include using sounds to confront an opposing inner force or for nurturing and healing a hurt feeling. An example could be that after a client has been through an experience of perhaps, pain, frustration, anger, being unsafe, or some such experience, they learn through gesturing and breathing to make the sound of their IT. This may be experienced and seen as an invading, encroaching or annoying inner dynamic. The sound becomes the externalized expression of the IT and offers both the client and the therapist a 'sound perspective' of what the IT is like. Sound is only one way for clients to express IT in a Psychophonetics session. IT can also be expressed through clay sculpture, drawing, writing and as we have seen, with the hands and body through gestures.

The sounds are powerful inasmuch as they become 'living external expressions' of the experience emanating from the clients soul. Rudolf Steiner, from whom Psychophonetics was inspired, indicated that there are about thirty two pure Universal sounds with thousands of sound combinations. These Universal sounds are the basis of our everyday language around the world. These pure Universal sounds[13] are what form many of the world's alphabets.

An example of how sound can be used in Psychophonetics:

If I were to Gesture the feeling of being downtrodden or suppressed by something or someone, I might express that experience with the support of the sound *"duh"* with a hand gesture of pushing downwards with the palms of my hands towards the floor. Together with the hands and the *"duh"* sound I would be externally expressing

---

13 'Speech and Drama' by Rudolf Steiner. Trans: M. Adams (19 lectures, Dornach, Sept 1924). Steiner Books, Anthroposophic Press

the inner experience or feeling of the IT that I feel or experience is doing the suppressing. I would be expressing that force through my soul feeling with a soul gesture.

You can try this out for yourself.

Say *"duh"* as you push downwards with the palms of your hands towards the floor. Do it several times – say "duh–duh–duh" and as you do, push, push, push with your hands at the same time. What do your feet want to do when you say *"duh"*? Allow them to move naturally and in a way that feels right for them. Allowing the body to express itself freely is all part of the process.

Try sounding *"mmmmmm"* and see what you experience. Sense how your hands naturally want to move and let them do so. Try *"ahhhhh"* and *"f–f–f–f–f"* and *"t–t–t–t–t"*. Sounding is a wonderful and creative way to get used to expressing ourselves and can be lots of fun.

In the case of the client Jim, he found a sound to express what was inhibiting him from being in his power as a twelve year old. As with many cases, when using sound in a Psychophonetics session, a counter, more protective, defensive sound is often required to counteract the invading, more negative, suppressing or inhibiting sound or force. By finding a powerful, protective and counteractive sound, Jim was able to create his own clear space to keep out the invading force. The therapist mimics this sound, verbally offering it back to the client as a way for them to learn how to counteract, release or overcome the opposing force which helps to stop IT from getting (back) into their body or space.

Old and unconscious experiences can trigger us at any time. By becoming more conscious of these experiences, they begin to lose their power over us and by choosing to engage in and use the sound and gesture work it will enable us to change and restore our 'I' presence more easily.

Over time clients become much more confident and comfortable with expressing sounds. A memory of the sensations, movement and sounds used in the sessions become 'locked in' to the client's memory and etheric body, so that any future experience or challenge of a similar nature can be more easily remembered and dealt with.

The following story of Frank (not his real name) gives an understanding of the power of sound and why I do not prescribe specific sounds for people in a therapeutic setting:

I was facilitating a workshop and introducing sound meditation to the group. I had brought along my Tibetan Singing Bowl and was sounding it during part of a meditation. After we had completed the meditation, I asked everyone how it had been for them; naively thinking that the sound of the singing bowl would be uplifting and pleasant for everyone. Everyone except Frank had enjoyed it. For him, it reminded him of the years he had spent in a nuclear submarine off the shores of Soviet Russia. The sound of the bowl was a cause of alarm and unpleasantness for him. This was a big lesson for me about using sound. Observing how different sounds have different meanings and seeing the affect that this had on Frank was very valuable for me.

This, and many other stories that I have heard, is good reason why I don't prescribe sounds. As Psychophonetics practitioners, we support the client to find the right sounds for their experience, which is much more empowering for them anyway.

If you had to express a sound for how you are feeling *Right Now*, what sound would that be? Go on – don't be shy ... go ahead and move and gesture as you make your sounds. Go on let it out!

For more professional therapeutic work in this area, I recommend that you work with a qualified (Psychophonetics) practitioner. You can check out more on Psychophonetics by going to the website. See the information at the back of the book.

In my work as a Psychophonetics practitioner and also in much of my other work in personal and professional development, I often use artistic and creative expression as a tool for supporting people. Even in my business coaching I find that by bringing in some form of art or creative expression people get more out of the process and get to understand and do things on a deeper, more engaging level.

Chapter Fifteen

Artistic and Creative Expression

Sculpting with clay

I love to express my creativity and one of my favourite ways to do this is to work and create using clay. The process of allowing my energy, thoughts, emotions, feelings and intuition to form into something solid and tangible through clay is a wonderful experience and I would highly recommend that you do some clay work to support you on your journey. It is easy enough to buy clay. For about twenty five dollars you can buy a ten kilo block of clay from a clay supply shop, art supplier or even perhaps from a local school if they will let you have some. It is a good idea to keep some clay at home for those moments when you feel inspired to be creative or feel stuck and need to move through something.

I keep my clay in the garage where it is a bit cooler, that way the clay stays fresher for much longer. Your block of clay and your sculptures and forms will stay soft as long as they are kept wrapped in plastic and kept out of the air. This means that pieces can be reworked at any time.

A good way to start with clay work, if you have not done much or any before, is to take a lump of clay that is nice and comfortable and easy to work with. A piece of clay about the size of a tennis ball or an orange is generally about right for smaller sculptures. When you have the clay in your hands, begin to mould it slowly into a sphere or ball shape. You might like to close your eyes for this and get a sense of what it feels like. By doing this you will enter into a process of connecting with your senses on a deeper level, both externally and internally.

Once you have the sphere completed (and it doesn't have to be perfect), you can then sculpt whatever it is you would like to create.

To stay with the theme of the book, why not sculpt yourself as you are *Right Now*, as the Present You and just as you did with the pencils or crayons earlier allow the process to unfold as freely as you can. It does not have to be the shape of your face or body. Allow it to be abstract and express it as freely as you can – try to feel it rather than think about it.

Once you have completed the Present You sculpture you can put it next to your Present You drawing and observe the similarities and/or differences. This will give another image and a deeper understanding of who you are. This new perspective will help to give you a greater sense of how you are, physically, emotionally, mentally and spiritually.

Using clay can be very healing.

A few years ago my cousin from England was staying with me and was having a severe bout of migraine. After some discussion we decided to do some clay work to help her relieve the pain. I prompted her to push her pain and emotions into the clay to see what difference it would make. After about ten minutes her migraine had totally disappeared!

Where Am 'I' Right Now?

Whilst working in South Africa as a biodynamic consultant and trainer I facilitated several clay workshops, working on deepening the understanding of plants. I also spent time with some of the farm workers doing personal development work which incorporated working with clay. During one such workshop the male farm workers used the clay to express some of their emotions and I suggested that they take some clay home with them and use it if they felt any strong emotions arising during the evening as I knew that a few of the men attending the workshop had been pushing their wives around. The next morning two of the men told me that they had used the clay to diffuse their anger and had managed not to hit their wives. With further psychotherapeutic and counselling work on the farm, the domestic violence was reduced. As demonstrated with these stories, clay can be used in many ways and can be a very useful way for people to express and even heal themselves.

Other shapes I like to make during clay workshops are some of the platonic solids. Platonic solids are shapes in 3D. All the edges in a platonic solid are of equal length and all the angles are of equal measure and all the faces on each shape are of equal shape and size.

If you would like to explore these platonic solids, you might like to work with the clay to create and form a cube, which is the easiest of the platonic solids to make. You can then work your way up to forming a tetrahedron, or even perhaps one of the other more complicated shapes such as an icosahedron. With each one of these shapes it is good to begin by making the sphere first and working on from there. I find that forming a sphere has a calming and centering affect that helps me to settle into the process more easily.

The Platonic Solids

1. A Tetrahedron
Four triangular faces, four vertices, and six edges[14]

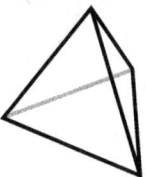

2. A Cube
Six square faces, eight vertices, and twelve edges

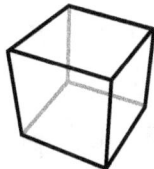

3. An Octahedron
Eight triangular faces, six vertices, and twelve edges

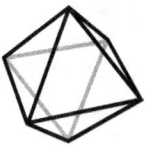

4. A Dodecahedron
Twelve pentagonal faces, twenty vertices, and thirty edges

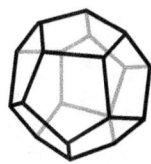

---

14 A 'vertex' (plural-vertices) is a corner; an 'edge' joins one vertex with another; and a 'face' is an individual surface.

5. **An Icosahedron**
Twenty triangular faces, twelve vertices, and thirty edges

It is so easy for me to get caught up in a kind of time warp when doing clay work and I can easily lose track of time. I really enjoy the process of working with clay and love to look at the final result, sometimes many hours after starting. Like other offerings and exercises suggested in this book, working with clay will give you a deeper understanding of where you are *Right Now* in your life if you choose to work with it.

Clay work can be lots of fun, so please, do go out and buy a big block of clay. This can be a wonderfully creative thing for all family members to do, from young to old and it is especially good fun for couples. Some amazing sculptures can be formed when done together as a couple.

For example, you can choose a theme, such as 'Love', and sculpt a piece together with this word in mind. Doing clay work in silence, or with some soothing music playing in the background is particularly enjoyable.

Arleen and I facilitate 'The Naked Truth' couples workshops and retreats and it is always interesting to observe couples doing the creative clay exercises together and observing what emotions come up for them in the process, especially when the couples are asked to reverse roles; where we ask the more dominant sculptor to become more passive and the more passive sculptor to become more dominant. This dominant versus passive combination is common

Artistic and Creative Expression

for many couples and bringing it out in clay work is very revealing. Eventually it becomes very rewarding for couples as they get to see how they play out their roles in the relationship.

An exercise for couples.

Set up a space where you will not be interrupted. Choose a time frame to work in that works for you. I would suggest at least thirty minutes and choose a word such as 'Love', 'Peace' or 'Intimacy' to work with. Take a large clump of clay and place it on a table or bench where you and your partner have free access to it from all sides and begin moulding the clay with your chosen word or phrase in mind. Allow your feelings, rather than your intellectual mind to guide and direct your hands. This exercise is wonderful to do in silence, with no conversation. Some soft music in the background can also be good.

Whilst doing this exercise be aware of the feelings and emotions that come up for you, especially as you begin to experience your partner changing parts of the clay that you have created. If one of you pokes a hole or squeezes a part of the clay that the other has created, just experience what happens. The aim of the exercise is to open up your awareness to what is going on in your soul as you do it and to deepen your connection as a couple.

You can stop after the allocated time or negotiate more time. Once the sculpture is complete you can let it dry, get it fired or place it out in the garden for the elements to take care of.

Where Am 'I' Right Now?

Sometimes it is not all plain sailing – stuff does come up when doing process work and it is good to be prepared for it. If you wish to take this further and experience a facilitated process then check out our couples workshops.

One thing that I would really like to emphasize in this book is the activity of being creative. We all have creative juices inside ready to be released. We often just need to find a way for your creative juice tap to be turned on, if it has not been turned on already.

We can choose to be creative in so many different ways. Some people struggle with the idea of being creative and yet, we are continually being creative every moment of the day with our thoughts, feelings, movement, sound, speech, meals, options, mess, children, pollution … We actually do lots of creating!

"*Yeah but I am not creative*" people often say to me. "*I cannot draw, paint, sculpt, act or write poetry, sing, play a musical instrument or cook*". "*Well*" I say to them, "*the only thing that stops you is the trying – so why not pick up a pencil, a crayon or a piece of clay and just allow it to unfold – and remember, it does not have to be perfect!*"

Being creative is not about getting it right and being perfect; it is a process. It is an unfolding of our potential and a way to express ourselves. It is a way to be in touch with our inner soul forces. Being creative is about letting ourselves be open to new possibilities and unleashing our unconscious. Often it is about taking a risk and exploring new territories and expanding our horizons.

One way in which I express my artistic creativity is with the didgeridoo. As well as playing and teaching the art of playing the didgeridoo I really enjoy making them, especially with pieces of hollowed out timber that I have found myself out in the bush. Creating new DVD's on *How to Play the Didgeridoo* and *Aligning and Healing the Chakras with the Didgeridoo and the Gongs* has been a very enjoyable and creative process.

Starting any new (creative) endevour can be a challenge and I remember when first playing the didgeridoo that it was a challenge and a struggle to get it all happening. I watched other people playing like masters and felt very awkward and at times I felt very intimidated. As I advanced my playing skills, I became more confident, creative and expressive and the more I practiced, the more competent and confident I became. It took courage, determination and dedication to unleash my creative didgeridoo playing self, but it was a process I had to go through in order to master it. Now I consider myself a very good didgeridoo player and teacher.

There are so many ways in which we can be artistic and creative; such as painting, drawing, sculpting, writing, playing music, craft and modelling, face painting, kite making, landscaping, hairdressing, sewing, embroidering, website designing, cooking, baking, and even tattooing ... the list goes on.

Think of three things that you would like to be creative with *Right Now?* and write them down. Go on, write these three things down in your *Right Now* journal and see if you can commit to starting one of them this week. To support you in the process, write down the steps that you will need to take to begin and the things that you will need to actually do it. Write down what materials you will need and what time and space you will need to do it.

Example: To start my painting this week I will need to buy some colourful paints, paintbrushes, paper or canvas and set aside three hours on Thursday afternoon.

Once we begin to venture into being more artistically creative, we can then also begin to look at how we might become more creative in other areas of our life. This can open up the question Where Am 'I' *Right Now?* for many topics.

Most people like to do one or several of the following things: interact, communicate, socialize, form relationships, become intimate, enter into sexual activities, go to work or even perhaps have a vocation or passion of some sort to follow. In the next few chapters we will explore some of these topics and you will be able to evaluate and see where you are in each of these areas of your life. One topic that I love to be creative in is life purpose, vocation and work.

Chapter Sixteen

Where Am 'I' *Right Now* with my Vocation or Life Purpose

'A man's life is his work'. This is an old saying and to some degree, I believe that it is true. We very often associate ourselves with what we do for a job or vocation or life purpose and measure and connect ourselves with what we do. We often introduce ourselves to others in relation to what we do for a living, a wage or a salary. *"Hi, my name is Adrian and I am a Life Mastery Coach"*.

My counselling and psychotherapy teacher, Yehuda Tagar, the Principal of Persephone College, would often say to me; *"Adrian, if a man* (more generally than a woman) *comes to you for a counselling session with some sort of life issue, always ask him if he has a job or a vocation or even a life purpose. If he does not, then there is a very good chance that this is the major issue going on for him. All of the other issues that he presents to you will most likely stem from this"*.

Even if we have a job, we still may wish for the day when we begin our vocational work and follow our deeper passion or life purpose. Do you perhaps have a sense of doing something more in the world and if so, can you name it? Perhaps you do not have anything that comes to mind. Perhaps you are already living it.

Where Am 'I' Right Now?

Whatever your current situation is *Right Now*, take a moment to contemplate this next question.

If you woke up tomorrow morning with a magic wand in your hand and could spend the next six weeks doing anything that you liked, in terms of work, job or vocation, what would you wish for, what would you choose to do?

Write this down in your *Right Now* journal.

After answering this question, give yourself some time to reflect on it. See if you can get a greater sense of what your vocational calling is or might be. If you do not have one or are content with where you are in the workplace that is alright, this is just an exercise to check where you are *Right Now* to see if you are really are where you wish to be, from a more conscious decision making perspective.

When working with people, either individually or in the group coaching programs that I conduct, there is always a strong element on vocational or job satisfaction. We spend quite a considerable amount of time looking at what it is to be happy and content in our 'work'.

What I have come to realize for myself is that I have been quite content and happy in most work situations during my life, but there has always been a sense of wanting to be a coach, facilitator, trainer and writer somewhere in my being. This wanting started to knock louder and louder over the years and it has become more defined in me over the past ten years or so.

As I write and prepare to launch even further and deeper into my coaching, facilitating and training, I know that I am living close to my vocational dream. The skills and experiences acquired during my life have all been fuel for this burning passion – my inner fire and desire to present this work.

Looking back over your own life you will also see an accumulation of skills and experiences that, when all combined and put together, will support you in whatever it is that you have a passion to step into and do.

> **Don't just follow your dreams, go catch them, put them in your pocket and re-release them as realities.**

Much of what we learn in life is born out of what we experience from our childhood family and the family or families that we later form ourselves with our own children. Our family patterns, beliefs and habits really do make us into who we are and sometimes this is a good thing and at others times it is not quite so good.

Chapter Seventeen

Where Am 'I' *Right Now* in my Family Life?

Nowadays, with many families blended, separated or spread out across the world, it is often very challenging to get a sense of where and how we actually belong. Generally, being with our family was, and perhaps for many people, still is, a huge part of our development and learning. It is the place where we learn rules, beliefs, taboos, politics, secrets, tricks, how to wear different personality masks and learn how to socialize. We all fit into our own families in different ways depending on the order of our birth, our relationship with each family member and our ability or lack of ability to communicate, speak our truth and to truly be ourselves.

It is not always an easy question to answer, but I will ask it anyway. How do you fit into your family? How is it for you with your parents, siblings, extended family members, your children and your grandchildren? How do you relate to the people in your family and how do they relate to you?

Take a moment and think of your closest family member, the

one who you get along and bond with the most and then think of the person in your family who you get along with the least. What is it about these people in your family that keeps you connected, less connected or perhaps even disconnected? What are the relationships like with them all? Why is it that you have different feelings and interactions with various family members? What games do you play, what masks do you wear? What is really happening with the family dynamics?

When we begin to unravel these questions and insights we can learn to take more self-responsibility for our thoughts, feelings and actions around our families. With friends, we have a choice – we choose our friends depending on what we like or dislike about them. Most of our friends have something we require, like or yearn for. We choose to have certain friends in our lives because of their nature, their personality and their interactions with us. With family members, they are simply there in our lives and part of what we have been born into. We did not really have a choice about who our parents were or who our siblings would be. As children we are told by our parents that we must 'get on' with our siblings and other family members, regardless of whether or not we are compatible. With friends, we have a choice about who to be with – with family members we do not generally have this free choice.

Of course there are many esoteric or spiritual beliefs around karma and reincarnation and fate that connect us with certain people, including family members and I do not want to discount these beliefs. I am sure there are many reasons why we are in certain families at certain times of our lives. This topic may be something that you can explore further. I am taking a very basic view *Right Now* to help express and clarify how we communicate, interact and connect with our family members.

It may be worth spending some time looking at your own family patterns, relations, values and interactions to see what is going on. A good exercise for this is to draw a series of concentric circles on a piece of paper and write your name in the middle. Begin by writing down the names of your family members who are closest to you. These will go inside the first circle. Slowly work your way outwards and put the names of each family member according to your connection with each one of them. The closer your relationship is to them, the closer their name is to yours in the centre and the more distant you are from them, the further their name is from yours.

A friend of mine has a large photo-collage on her wall of all her family members. It is a beautiful reminder of the connection that she has with her large family.

You can also do this concentric circle exercise for evaluating your friendships to see where your friends fit into your life. You might like to keep these exercises private, so as not to upset anyone!

Once you have a clear picture of where each family member is on your family concentric circle chart, you can then look at individual relationships and see where they need some attention, some communication or perhaps some real letting go.

If you look back through your life you will observe that different family members meant different things to you at different times. Family members come in and out of our lives depending on what

Where Am 'I' Right Now in my Family Life?

we are doing, where we live, how well we communicate with them and how much we do or do not, allow them into our lives. Our old family patterns, issues, misunderstandings, upsets and beliefs are sometimes carried for many years. Old family rifts can go on for generations, to the point where nobody really knows any more what it was all about in the first place. Take a moment to reflect on where you can take some self-responsibility with your own family relationships. Where are you, *Right Now* with it all? What would you like to do and when and how will you attempt to do it?

Living in Australia, with most of my family in England, I do not get to see them as often as I would like. When I travel to England to see them every few years, I immediately become aware of how I am put into situations where I have to stand very much more present in my being if I am not to be drawn back into old negative or non-serving family patterns, beliefs and behaviours. Family get-togethers can easily draw me back into the family fold, back into places that I have not been in for a long time if I am not centred and standing fully in my 'I' presence.

What was it like the last time you had a family get-together or family reunion like a wedding, birthday party or such celebration? Did the behaviour of other family members surprise you or did you experience the same old thing? How was your own behaviour – did you play an interesting role too?

With my own family, I am alert to how I feel and act when communicating and meeting up with them. I am always surprised at how easy it is for me to fall into old family patterns and habits. As I do not drink alcohol or smoke pot it helps me to stay more focused and present and enables me to say and do pretty well anything I feel I need to do. If I feel or see a possible old family situation or family pattern arising I can, by being present to my thoughts, feelings and actions, defuse or change the course of action that has the potential to become uncomfortable or challenging for me or anyone else in the family. Family get togethers such as weddings and christenings and even funerals are places where old family feuds can resurface and cause chaos.

I have worked with many clients who have attempted to repair or improve their relationship with family members and in the process they have realized how incredibly powerful family dynamics can be. I remember facilitating and mediating a half day session with a man and his mother about their dysfunctional family dynamics. He was in his forties and she was in her seventies. Part of the family story that kept them at odds with one another was thirty years old! It took an afternoon of facilitating and mediating to finally tease out 'the story' and change the dynamics. It was a powerful session and very empowering for both the mother and her son. Letting go of a story that is over thirty years old is not an easy task, but lots of humour on this occasion helped us

Chapter Eighteen

Where Am 'I' *Right Now* in my Social Life?

It is at a young age that we learn our first social skills and the things that we learn set the course for many of the things that we do, think and feel when socializing. I am often amazed at how present day young children and teenagers, including my own children, hold themselves in conversation in my adult social circles. It certainly was not like that for me when I was a child. Yes, my parents socialised, but my inclusion in conversations with adults was nothing like it is for my own and other friend's children. I can sit at a table with six adults and six children from the ages of ten to eighteen and their input is not only heard, but also valued and respected.

As we are within our family lives, when in social settings with our friends and colleagues we also act out and play different roles with different masks to suit us and the moment. We have all learned to wear many hats, put on many faces and change our personalities frequently to wiggle our way through life and for much of the time we are totally unconscious of actually doing it. It takes commitment and energy to challenge ourselves to become more aware of the way in which we think, feel and act in the world and in our social life it is no different.

One thing that we often do in social settings, if we are not fully in our 'I' presence, is to go along for the ride even if we feel that it is not what we really want to do. There may be situations such as: a silly game is being played where you have to drink too much alcohol or there may be a place that everyone else wants to go to (like a strip club) that you do not like to go to yourself and yet you find yourself engaging in the activity despite not really wanting to.

Take a moment *Right Now* to remember a time when you just went along with whatever was going on in a social setting, but not really wanting to do it. How might you now learn how to challenge yourself to only do the things that really serve you and only do the things that you like to do socially, instead of just going along for the ride with the crowd?

Here is a story to share about this.

For many years I was a regular smoker of tobacco and marijuana, and then, when I was about twenty eight, I decided to stop. At the time, I was living in a small country hamlet where smoking marijuana and drinking alcohol was part of the weekend social gatherings. It was a big challenge for me to keep going along to these social gatherings once I had decided to stop smoking, as one of the main reasons for meeting up was to get stoned and or drunk. After a few weekends after making the decision to stop, I realized that I was getting more and more uncomfortable with my new situation of being a non-smoker, but was also aware that the others in my social circle were becoming uncomfortable with it too. By giving up I had changed the social paradigm that we had all been living and sharing for several years. I finally left this social group after someone in the group, rather than supporting me in my decision to give up, actually spiked my drink with some drugs. That was the end for me with that social group and it really helped me to re-define my values around supportive friendships.

Take a moment to see where you are *Right Now* with your own social life situation. Are you content? Do things need to be improved, changed or perhaps communicated in a new way? Do you need to step up or step out?

As with all of the exercises, ideas and suggestions in this book, it is all about – How you are *Right Now*? The focus of this book is to support, challenge and guide you to make more conscious choices in all areas of your life, physically, emotionally, mentally and spiritually. Family, friends, work and vocation, sexuality, health, fitness, hobbies and recreation are all areas we can explore and work with further. If we are consciously choosing to engage in a more holistic journey of discovery, transformation and personal empowerment, then I believe it is well worth our time and energy to explore and review all areas of our lives.

With the advent of social media it is so very easy to get caught up in on-line social activity and lose the real-life connections we have with people. I know people who spend hours on Facebook or playing fantasy games like Second Life or World of War-craft spending hours hidden away in their room and locked into their game-world and lessening or missing out on real human contact. This is becoming a very big issue, especially for young people. Many people, especially those of the younger generations, struggle to have more than a two minute conversation without having to check their mobile/smart phone. To engage socially is such an important part of human development and the techno-age of computers and suchlike really is challenging our whole fabric of society and if it is not put into some sort of order, especially with things like pornography, I feel that we will be paying the price for non-action for a very long time.

Connecting with other people is such a huge part of social skill building and a big part of what it is that makes us human-spiritual beings. When we begin to move away from these connections and interactions we may run the risk of losing our senses and feelings of intimacy.

Chapter Nineteen

Where Am 'I' *Right Now* with my Intimacy?

Intimacy is a difficult thing to define and put into words. It is something we generally feel rather than think about. Being intimate is generally linked to being in close contact and communication with someone whom we love – in a deep loving relationship.

A friend of mine once showed me these words that he had found in a book somewhere: Intimacy = In To Me See. To be intimate with someone often requires a deeper connection from within; from somewhere deep within our soul. For me, this interpretation describes this very well.

The dictionary definition of the word Intimate is: inward, internal, familiar friend, close. I would like to use the word intimate in a deeper, more specific way, in a way that we would use it to describe our relationship with a lover, partner or spouse.

I know we can be intimate with our mothers, fathers, brothers, sisters and close friends. However, for the purpose of this book, intimacy will be defined as: the feeling or experience we have when we are with our lover, partner or spouse, or with someone who is close enough for us to share our deepest thoughts, feelings, fantasies, desires, fears, doubts, needs, dreams and aspirations.

For me, intimacy in a relationship is a very special soul bonding process. It is a bond that is delicately woven with vulnerability, trust, love, respect, honour and a sense of sacredness. Being in a place of intimacy means I allow my partner, lover or spouse into my soul; into that most fragile and vulnerable part of my being.

Once this vulnerability, trust, respect or sacredness has been cracked, broken or violated, it is often very difficult to open it up and let the same or another person in again. The experience of having one's intimate space wounded can take years to repair and heal. Finding a way to enter into someone else's intimate space and also allowing someone into our own, is like a delicate careful dance, as step by careful step we move closer to one another until the doors of trust, respect, honouring and vulnerability are open wide enough for us to step inside.

When communication, sexuality and connection are intertwined with intimacy, something special evolves for couples. A bond is formed that is powerful and strong and even when people are 'going through their stuff' and times get tough between them, this intimate bond can help retain an aspect of sacredness, respect, honouring and trust. In couples counselling and coaching sessions, I see this very clearly with some of the couples who have formed it. Even though they come to see me about challenges or issues that they are facing in the relationship, their bond of intimacy is palpable. Sadly, most of the time, intimacy is not something that is taught alongside sexuality in our homes or education systems to our children and this is partly due to the fact that many couples (teachers and educators included) struggle to find or have this in their own relationships. When this is not experienced, seen or passed on to our next generations it can begin to get diminished and even lost.

I coach and counsel many people who struggle with intimacy in their lives. Sexuality is often far more prevalent in the bedroom than intimacy and it is often this lack of intimacy that drives couples apart. A soft intimate and affectionate touch, word or look can be a deep and powerful thing. When we are in touch with our own intimate nature we can be much more open with our feelings, thoughts, dreams, passions, fears and doubts and then share some of these with our partners.

Being intimate is something we generally have to work at. It is two-fold. Firstly, we have to learn to be intimate with ourselves and secondly, we have to learn to be intimate with our lover, partner or spouse. When we are in a process of self-talk and are kind to ourselves this is a form of intimacy. When we are nurturing ourselves, trusting ourselves, honouring ourselves and respecting ourselves this is being intimate with self. When we put a hand on our own heart when it has been hurt and gently stroke it, we are being intimate. When we do these things for someone else, that too is being intimate.

Take a moment to see where you are *Right Now* in terms of intimacy in your life.

How intimate are you with yourself? And if you have a partner, lover or spouse, how intimate are you both in the relationship? Take a moment to acknowledge all that you do have and do, or do not have and do, in your relationship with yourself and with other special people in your life. Write these things down and if you can, share them with your partner. Make time to discuss your thoughts and understandings and insights with your partner and make a commitment to take your intimacy to a new level.

Explore what intimacy means for you. A great way to explore this is by simply asking the question – Where Am 'I' *Right Now* with my sense of intimacy? And then seeking and finding the answers.

From sharing thoughts on intimacy, it is probably an obvious step to start talking about sexuality.

Chapter Twenty

Where Am 'I' *Right Now* with my Sexuality?

This is the section that many people will either jump to first after looking at the index or skip completely. SEX! SEX! SEX! This word conjures up many issues, comments, reactions, projections and jokes that it almost needs a book of its own. Sex *Right Now!* Wow that title would sell a few books!

For many people, sex is a challenging topic to fully embrace. It is a subject that is often overlooked, dismissed or hidden. Even though sex is a large part of our life, it seldom gets much serious attention or discussion. Sex seems to be something we participate in and then keep under the sheets (pun intended!) and kept secret. Unless the subject of sex is raised as a joke, it is not something that is very often talked about in every-day life – unless you are part of a Men's or Women's Group that have the courage to go there.

To give you an example of what I mean I would like to share a true story with you.

At a personal development weekend workshop that I attended we had to write down our ten favourite things. Out of the twenty five or so people in the room, I was the only person who wrote down the word Sex! In fact it was on the top of my list! As soon as I read it out to the group, many of the people in the room quickly wrote it on their list too! It was not in anyone's consciousness or if it was, perhaps they may have had some fear about writing it down. With

Where Am 'I' Right Now with my Sexuality?

me writing it down and expressing it, I felt as if I had helped pave the way for the others in the room to become more conscious about their love of sex and for them to be able to express it.

Why is this story so unusual? What is it about sex not being in our consciousness when it is something that most adults on the planet love to engage in? As we men know, and of which we are often reminded in both humorous and serious ways; men have sex on their minds all the time! – So why is it not common for men to write sex down as a top ten favourite? I have tested this theory out with similar test questions myself in Men's Groups and it is very rare for even men to write sex down on their list of ten favourite things. I love golf and footy too guys, but come on!

I would like for you to take a moment to consider your own connection to sex and sexuality. How does the word sex and the subject of sex, resonate with you? How often do you talk about sex? How often do you think about sex? How often do you engage in sex? Does sex play a big part in your life? Is it on your list of the top ten favourite things to do?

Supposing that you *can* write sex down on your list – how about taking it to the next level and writing down ten of your favourite sexual activities. Go ahead, be courageous and write down your top ten favourite sexual activities if you dare!

If we are to be authentic and honest with ourselves in our journey, we have to, at some point, address issues around sex and become more blunt and honest with ourselves, and perhaps with others, about our views, thought and feelings about sex and sexuality. When we begin to free ourselves from our old taboos, fears and misconceptions around sex, often gained during our teenage years, we can then begin to engage more fully and honestly with the topic of sex and perhaps the very act of sex itself!

I believe healthy and open discussion about sex with our sexual partners deepens the bond between us. It allows a certain freedom to arise and from this place a deeper trust and understanding can be formed.

If we know what our partner's views, inhibitions, requirements, needs, perceptions and taboos are within the sexual journey that we share together, we then have the knowledge to make the art of sexuality more comfortable, enjoyable and real for them as well as for ourselves. Sexuality is an art. It is something to study, to work with and to master. Like any art, it takes time and practice to be in a position of mastery and the only way to become a master, is to practice.

There is much information on sex, especially on the internet which allows it to be freely available in many forms, from crass pornography to beautiful sacred/Tantric practices. People choose to read, view and engage in a wide range of sexual activities and acts from somewhere or other between these two polarities and I believe that it is important in any sexual relationship to know what and where our own and our partner's, comfort zones are in all of this.

Many people choose to use pornography to spice up their sexual life. People, including the younger generation, can watch pornography very freely via their computers and mobile phones and after only a short time can become very addicted to watching it. It concerns me deeply that the younger generations have such easy access to it. Many of the boys I have worked with in schools have told me that they watch 'porn' on a regular basis. The imaginations and images formed in their minds from their exposure to pornography is a far cry to what many of us know as something sacred and beautiful. I often say to the teenage boys that I work with, *"As you will experience at some point, movie sex is okay but the real thing is better"*. Boys in particular, but many girls too, now base their own sexual wants and needs around what they see from the pornography that they watch. This can become very confusing and misleading for them in terms of learning and understanding what it is to be a sensual and caring lover.

For the partners of people who base their needs around pornography, but do not have the same needs or fantasies themselves, this can become very challenging and difficult. Relationships can become challenged when pornography enters a couple's sex life and it may require some professional support to work through it. Because of the work I do as a counsellor and psychotherapist, I meet many men in their thirties, forties and older who have porn-addictions and many of them tell me that the relationship that they have with their partner is not very good.

Generally, it is men who tend to become more fixated with pornography. When they do, their sexual partners can, in the mind of the man, be reduced from being a loving sexual partner to his living, walking and performing porn star fantasy or illusion. I am not saying that fantasy should not be part of anyone's sex life, what I am trying to convey is the powerful energy and havoc and potential danger that pornography can bring to relationships. The topic of pornography certainly needs to be mentioned and discussed further in our schools and in our communities as it is already having a huge negative impact on people's lives, especially younger people trying to come to grips with their own sexual beliefs, understandings and relationships.

It might be worth exploring your own beliefs, thoughts and experiences around pornography so that you have a clearer understanding about your own (hidden) views. How do you feel about it and how do you feel about your own children being exposed to it? And for you, at what level do sex scenes on the screen or in literature become pornographic?

This topic is really worth exploring as it is such a hidden and often taboo aspect of our world. The pornography industry is growing at a very rapid rate. What do you think about pornography being freely available on the internet and how are your powers of will against clicking buttons on your keypad that lead you directly to sites showing explicit sexual/ pornographic acts? Are you truly able to resist clicking that button on your computer or phone that leads to porn?

As I do research around sex education and the effect of pornography, I am amazed at the amount of explicit content freely available on the internet. It can be a challenge to steer through the maze of sex sites to find educational and topic related sites that sit within my own standards or acceptable levels of what sexual education is, as opposed to pornography. How we, as parents, teachers and therapists, work with young children and teenagers certainly needs to change if we are to support and navigate them into adult life with a deeper and more sacred sense of what sex and sexuality should be.

This pornography epidemic certainly needs an antidote – and that antidote is truly overdue! If you have a child, there is a huge chance that your teenager *will* be watching some form of pornography on the internet by the time they are thirteen or fourteen! Sadly the statistics prove it. Pornography is so easy to access and such a thrilling and tantalizing thing for people to watch that it is hard to stop it. Trying to stop children from watching pornography is like telling a small child not to put their hand in the open lolly jar when left alone in a lolly shop – it is simply almost impossible for them not to do so. The energy of pornography is powerful. Pornography addiction is, in my opinion, as addictive as the strongest drugs. The immense astral pull that IT has over the 'I' is immense. When we understand that children and teenagers (and some adults) are yet to have their 'I' fully incarnated, it becomes scaringly obvious of how easy it is for them to succumb to the energy of pornography.

I would like to bare my soul and share a very personal story with you.

A couple of years ago I was out shopping for a few things and needed to use the local public toilet. Up against the wall, next to the urinal there was a portable DVD player. I picked it up thinking that I would place a small 'found' flyer near the toilet and return the DVD player to its owner. Back at home I opened the machine to find that there was a disc inside. On pushing the play button I was shocked to see some very heavy pornography playing on the screen. It was a movie with two on one sex (two men and one woman). I had watched pornography in the past, but not quite as shocking as what I was now watching. Did I turn it off? Yes – but only after watching for a few minutes – and it was not easy to press the stop button. I then went about my business of whatever it was that I had to do that day, continually thinking about what I had seen, but my curiosity got the better of me and back I went again to watch the movie. Standing in my kitchen I switched the movie on and watched for another few minutes – I was both enthralled and repulsed at the same time – the battle of my astral self and my 'I' was on! It took all of my inner strength to pull the disc from the DVD player and smash it! It was a familiar old battle for me – the battle of addiction. Seeing the shattered disc on the kitchen floor was a huge relief.

It was a deep reminder for me of my time as an addict with drugs and alcohol. I really got a sense and an experience again of how powerful the astral aspect of our being can be. If it was such a battle for me; a strong minded and strong willed man, how can we really expect teenagers to overcome this immensely powerful force?

Sacred sexuality

Now let's move on to something that is, for me, much more beautiful. Sacred sexuality is an art that is followed and practiced by tens of thousands of people across the world, generally in the East. It is often referred to as Tantric sexuality. There is a lot of information available on the subject and in countries like India and Tibet the art of Tantra is quite a common practice. The path of Tantra is more than just sex; it is more about bringing sacredness into one's life on many levels, physically, emotionally, mentally and spiritually through doing things such as yoga and meditation, often connecting to the Chakras to deepen the energy flow.

In the more rational, mainstream western world, sacred or tantric sex is not so widely known or practiced as it is not part of how we have been educated. For many of us, sex education was delivered at school or at home in a cold un-sacred scientific way, perhaps dispersed with jokes or mocking and/or from reading sex magazines or watching pornography.

Essentially, sacred sex is about joining in union with more than just the physical side of sexuality in mind – it is about connecting to a higher energy, an energy or experience that could be called spiritual. It is about harnessing and using our energy to heighten and even prolong sexual activity. For people who practice and use tantric sex, the physical ejaculation and orgasm for the man is often seen as something to prolong or to not even experience in some cases. With some practice, it is possible for men to heighten and prolong their sexual pleasure by controlling their need to ejaculate and also giving more time and focus for the woman to enjoy her orgasms or ejaculations. This is a far cry from the sex education many of us were given. If we could only educate ourselves and our children worldwide to have beautiful healthy, sacred tantric sex, I can only wonder what the world would be like.

Like many other topics in this book, sacred sexuality is a topic that can be further studied and practiced. Sacred sexuality, as we have come to see, can be a very spiritual experience and is only a part of a whole and complete spiritual path that we can explore and engage in, if we choose too.

Chapter Twenty One

Where Am 'I' *Right Now* in my Spiritual Life?

In this chapter I will attempt to distinguish the spiritual world, from what I call the astral world. I take my knowledge from my many years of experience with spiritual investigation and from working with hundreds of people as a counsellor and facilitator.

In the astral world, that place of the soul where we activate and use our senses, we can easily evoke images and feelings and experiences that may seem spiritual to us if we do not have a reference point or an experience of the spiritual world to gauge it from.

In my experience from using drugs in the past and from spending over twenty years researching, investigating and practicing a rich spiritual path, I feel as if I can speak with some authority on this. Mucking around within this realm of astrality with drugs whilst believing it is the spiritual realm can be dangerous on many levels. When people have these astral experiences and see and experience things and beings that they often do not recognise or understand, it can be the first step to getting in too deep, and unfortunately, in some cases, can lead to people losing their minds and sense of reality.

In my experience and understanding the spiritual world is generally not accessible when under the influence of drugs unless one is carefully guided by someone who has the wisdom and training to guide us there. In many ancient cultures, this was the role of the hierophant or the medicine man or shaman. He/she would guide the initiate safely over the threshold and back again, ensuring a safe passage. Sadly, in today's culture these people are rare and without them people try to access realms of consciousness and spiritual connection that are far beyond their reach or comprehension and they can get into all sorts of trouble as they are ill prepared for what they may face.

As a guide I would say that if you are having feelings and seeing bright, moving or psychedelic colours whilst on your out of body experience, then you are most likely in the astral realm. And if you have not passed through the 'Gates of the Guardian's'[15], then you are definitely not fully prepared, ready and equipped to be in the spiritual realm.

Coming to grips with what spirituality really means to you will most likely be one of the greatest quests that you take in your life if you choose to embark on such a challenging journey and having some background understanding of the many pitfalls and dangers is often a good policy to have. Many people 'lose the plot' from experiencing too much too soon and without having someone to support and guide them along the way. I do not want to be an alarmist, but I do know from my own, and from observing other's experiences, that these dangers are very real. I know several people who had non-drug related spiritual awakenings, and had they not been taken in by people who understood such things, they would most certainly have ended up in a psychiatric unit.

When awakening to life and connecting to things that have some spiritual meaning, some of the fundamental questions we ask

---

15 There are, in esoteric work regarding stepping over into the realm of Spirit, two Guardians in place to protect us and bar our entry if we are not yet prepared and ready for such a journey. These guardians are known as the Lesser and Greater Guardians. For more information read Rudolf Steiner's *Knowledge of the Higher Worlds*.

Where Am 'I' Right Now?

through life are: Who am I? Is there a God? Is there life after death? And perhaps for some – What is my true purpose? Spirituality really is a quest; a question. It is a quest to know ourselves and to know about the world in which we live. It leads us to ask questions about the hidden and the unknown; like God and the Universe.

As we go through life we ask many questions and find ourselves on quests, explorations and studies in search for the answers. One way to search for our deeper answers is to step onto a spiritual path or find and join a spiritual group, faith or religion. There are a myriad of spiritual pathways to choose from. The question is; which one?

I would like for you to pause for a moment and ask yourself – Where Am 'I' *Right Now* with my own spiritual journey?

Take a few minutes to write a few things in your journal. Write down what your own spiritual path is (if you have one) and write down a few of the values that you hold about this path. Add a few words about why this spiritual path is important to you.

This writing exercise will give you a clearer indication of where you are *Right Now* on your own spiritual path.

Of course, in reality, we are all on a spiritual journey from the moment of our birth right through to the day that we die. If you recognise or acknowledge that you are on a spiritual journey of some kind *Right Now* in your life, it means you are probably searching for some answers. It probably means that you have a belief, a hope or a confirmation that there is a dimension which extends past your ordinary earthbound experience. Generally spirituality implies that we are on some kind of path or journey which moves and goes beyond the physical.

Tapping into this other dimension or spiritual world is something that people have done for tens of thousands of years. No matter what path we follow, there will be a need to have an understanding of it if we are not to become like sheep and just follow someone else's belief, dogma or words. Being present and conscious means we also have to be clear about our own thoughts, beliefs and understandings and know what it is we are following or stepping into.

I have a theory or an understanding that I would like to share with you with regard to following a spiritual practice. See if it makes sense to you.

When we begin a spiritual practice of any kind, there are always the basics to learn first. The terminology is generally very important so we can engage with others who are on the same or similar path. We can then discuss our interests, ideas, beliefs and philosophies with some understanding and clarity. We also learn the basic tenants and principles of the path we have chosen to explore and study and also perhaps learn some of the associated texts, verses, lectures and meditations.

Once we begin following, studying and practicing a spiritual discipline we come to see and experience that there are certain steps or levels that have to be taken along the way to gain more wisdom, knowledge and understanding.

Where Am 'I' Right Now?

To move from one step or level to the next requires a certain amount of study, work, dedication and discipline. Each step prepares the student to move on to the next step or level of experience and understanding. If the step that we are on and striving to master, has not been sufficiently understood and experienced, then there is generally little point of moving on to the next one. Missing or not completing a step thoroughly is a little bit like trying to go from kindergarten through to university and missing primary school or high school. There is a system to follow in order to advance from one level to the next in any kind of study and spirituality *is* a study.

If we study and practice a certain path and at the end of that basic study (say stage one) we move to another path or discipline and study the basics of that one, then we would be back at base level again, back at stage one. We can do many years of spiritual study and practice and still only have the basics if we chop and change disciplines. All that happens then is that we end up going from basics to basics to basics …

If you can continue with one spiritual discipline or practice year after year, you will find that you will advance in knowledge and understanding more solidly and the rewards and outcomes will start to become evident to you and to others around you by the way in which you think, feel, act and behave in the world.

Let us not kid ourselves, spiritual study and practice is challenging and difficult work!

Spirituality is very much about self-mastery. It is about striving for and having complete faith and unconditional love or whatever else it is that draws you onto your spiritual path. Whatever it is that you are striving for or mastering, you will need to strengthen your patience, determination, courage, clarity, will, staying power, sense of surety and your sense of self.

As with any study or challenge it is good to have some guidelines to work with and spirituality is no exception. I have added some recommendations from my own experience as a guide line. For simplicity, we will call them steps one to ten.

Ten recommended steps for the path of spiritual development

1. Make a start and choose just *one* path or discipline.

2. Learn and understand the basic language and terminology of your chosen path.

3. Seek guidance and support from others on the same or similar path.

4. Make a commitment to study regularly.

5. Question everything. Do not believe it just because someone else said or wrote it.

6. Take each step methodically, cautiously and wisely.

7. Complete each step or level of attainment and understand it well before moving on to the next step or level.

8. Practice, test and use your new learning in the world.

9. Remember that there is always another step. There is always more to learn and know. Don't rest on your laurels!

10. Remember to refer back on your journey at times to determine and measure where you are *Right Now*.

My main spiritual teacher and mentor for over twenty years has been Rudolf Steiner. He gave many indications on how to journey effectively, safely and steadily along a spiritual path and he offered many exercises to do this. In his book, *Knowledge of the Higher Worlds*[16] (Chapter Five), he named these as The Seven Conditions of Spiritual Development.

---

16 A more modern version of this book is titled: "Requirements for Esoteric Training".

These seven conditions translated in my words are:

1. Developing our wellbeing. Taking responsibility for our physical, emotional, mental and spiritual health.

2. Developing our empathy. Seeing and understanding other people from the inside, from their position in life.

3. Developing our understanding that our inner world (soul life) is as real as the outer (physical) world.

4. Distinguishing between our own truth and the truth of others and respecting both. Developing the knowing of our own inner truths.

5. Developing our ability to move from planning to completion. Developing the will to complete.

6. Developing our sense of gratitude. Appreciating everything in our lives.

7. Finding consistency. Working with all of the above six conditions together.

As I have expressed previously in this book, there are many spiritual paths and disciplines to choose from and to follow. My recommendation is that you find one that suits you and stick with it for as long as you can, so that you can at least get beyond the basics.

It is like being an apprentice to begin with, where others with more wisdom and experience can help to guide us in the early years of our development and learning. I would say that two or three years of being an apprentice is a good time frame to learn the basics and is long enough to get more knowledge of the spiritual realms before venturing out by yourself. Once the basics have been covered it is then time to move on to more advanced learning's and levels. Time and time again I meet and observe people who have leapt in with little or no spiritual training or understanding, and claim to be this or that master or spiritual expert or channel or medium, and time and time again I observe these people floundering, getting lost or getting caught up in their own ego. This is especially undermining for the people who *have* done the necessary work and devote their time to be spiritual practitioners. I know some very good spiritual teachers and practitioners and know some very shonky and shady ones too. At the end of the day it is all about self-evaluation and honesty and if people step into realms of spirituality that they cannot handle, they will eventually learn their lessons, hopefully not too harshly.

I have known people step into and over their level of ability and knowledge and get very lost for quite some time and it took the skill and patience of very experienced spiritual practitioners to 'bring them back' and stabilise them. The spiritual realm has many levels, and like scuba diving you have to learn that each level or depth brings new challenges and dangers. Diving down into the ocean without any scuba diving training would be stupid and dangerous and for me, this is no different with spiritual investigation and study.

In my opinion, the basic disciplines and understandings in any spiritual path or practice should include:

Regular meditation, regular study of texts and mantras, guidance from a master or competent guide, a basic knowledge of the spiritual realms and the beings that reside there, a common spiritual language, a sharing with others on a similar path to get other perspectives and a rigorous and regular daily dose of spiritual development through practical exercises (like this book is offering). Oh, and a very good sense of humour!

To foster a healthy spiritual life we generally have to change a few of our thoughts, feelings and actions, especially towards others. It may mean that we have to make a few changes to the way in which we spend our time and energy and perhaps even our money. Living a spiritual life that has meaning and authenticity can be a challenge. People have many versions and beliefs on what spirituality is and often have many different ways to express it. I find that what is of most importance to me is to be clear and sure about my own path and to walk it with as much knowledge, responsibility and awareness as I can.

There are many components to living a spiritual life and one big part is about taking more care of ourselves; physically, emotionally, mentally and spiritually.

Chapter Twenty Two

Self-Care

This chapter is all about you focusing on you in a caring and loving way. This is all about you learning to fully embrace and accept yourself for the beautiful, talented, intelligent and courageous person that you are. It is all about honouring yourself in a new way. In essence it is about self-care.

Learning to love ourselves and to really honour the amazing being that we are can be a challenge. Standing tall in the world is not always easy. Learning how to fully love ourself may take some practice if we are not good at doing so already.

There are many levels of love and as this chapter is about you focusing on you, the first thing that I would like to ask is: How much do you love your physical self – your physical body?

When you stand naked in front of a mirror, wearing no clothes, make-up, jewellery or anything else, how much do you love what you see? Can you truly accept yourself for who you are on a physical level, without any of the usual adornments?

If this is a new concept for you and standing naked in front of a mirror and seeing yourself reflected back is something you have not really done before, then it can be a terrifying ordeal if you are not already in a comfortable place about acknowledging and loving yourself. This challenge may be scary for you, as it will reveal how you really feel about yourself. It will give you a sense of where you might need to focus your attention.

The fashion and cosmetics industries hone in on this 'sense of not being good enough' or 'sense of worthlessness' and make billions of dollars from it every year. Cosmetic companies spend millions on advertising with this knowledge that people feel bad about how they look without any makeup on their faces. Lipstick, foundation, blusher, nail polish, hair-spray, deodorant, shampoo and conditioner, hair dyes, fake tans, eye shadow, mascara, wigs, skin bleaching and liposuction are some of the things helping people to feel beautiful and loved. So, how are you without any of these things when you stand totally naked in front of a mirror?

Yes, you are one step ahead of me ... you know what I am going to ask of you, right?

Off you go then! Go and stand in front of that mirror and give yourself the test. Ask yourself the question – Where Am 'I' *Right Now* in terms of my comfort zone and my self-love and acceptance of who I am physically?

When you do this, scan your body from top to bottom (excuse the pun) and be aware of which parts of your body you like and which parts you are not so happy with. Part of this process will be to acknowledge what needs to be changed in terms of your beliefs, thoughts and feelings about yourself and your image of whom and what you are. It will also highlight what you may need to address and change about your physical body if you are not happy with it.

Where Am 'I' Right Now?

If it needs attention you can choose to make some new choices. You may feel that you need to lose or gain some weight, get fitter or even just cut your toe nails to make you feel better.

Being comfortable with who we are can be a challenge. The physical aspect of ourselves is the most obvious and as we stand in front of the mirror we get to see ourselves very clearly. It is easy to wear a mask to cover up our fears, doubts, guilt, shame, embarrassment, or confusion. It is easy to walk through life hiding our true-self. Being authentic and real can be a challenge. Being honest and real about who we are and what we stand for in life can be one of our greatest challenges in being true and present.

Speaking our truth, expressing our true emotions and feelings and living our lives in a way that truly expresses who we are is one of the keys to leading and living a full and contented life. This is all part of caring and loving ourselves. Being caring and loving towards ourselves means that we have to learn and practice the art of self-love and self-care in a very conscious way. We have to be forever vigilant with ourselves in every thought, feeling and action and take the time and the effort to address areas in our lives that need to improve.

This exercise will give you a good indication about how you think and feel about yourself.

When facilitating personal development events, especially Men's

Circles, I frequently work with this exercise. It is called Honouring Self. It involves writing down words of honour. I ask each person in the group to write down twenty words that honour them. In many cases it is the men that struggle most to do this; much more so than women. Try it for yourself. Write down twenty honouring words that you would use to honour you. Try to do it in less than five minutes and see how you fare.

Example:

I am:

1. Loving

2. Creative

3. Intelligent

4. ...

20. Friendly

I trust that this exercise gave you a few feel good moments. See if you can make a new list every week or start a list where you add a new honouring word every day – forever!

After over two decades of working with people in personal, professional and spiritual development, I would say that the art of communication is by far the most challenging of all the topics that we have to deal with. A big part of self-love and self-care is about being conscious and awake to the way in which we communicate with ourselves and with other people.

Chapter Twenty Three

The Art of Communication

Verbal communication only accounts for about five – ten percent of our total communication. Our facial expressions and our eye and body movements and gestures and much more make up the other ninety percent. If you take a moment to consider this fact you will see what a fascinating and astounding piece of information this is.

Our way of communicating with one another is triggered by many components of human make up and behaviour. There are many methods which we can explore and use to improve our communication skills. Much of my own study and research in communication has been driven and guided from my connection to the work of Rudolf Steiner. As with many other areas of human-spiritual development, he gave many indications and teachings on this topic too. The book *Speech and Drama* by Rudolf Steiner is well worth reading.

If you try communicating with someone with your eyes closed or with your hands held tight by your side or by trying not to move your eyes, you will get quite a clear sense of how we communicate with each other with more than just our words. Oftentimes, we believe that we are communicating clearly with someone only to find that what we thought or believed we said was not interpreted in that way at all. Oh, what a surprise! Our different, unique and often clumsy ways of communicating are often confusing for others, even for people who supposedly speak the same language.

People who tend to communicate more strongly through their intellectual faculty, through their analytical left brain, may find it challenging and difficult to communicate easily with someone who communicates more dominantly from their right sided, more creative brain. Of course, that is also true the other way around.

One useful skill to learn to help you to communicate more effectively is to try to be more in touch and in union with the way in which the other person is trying to communicate with you. Being more focused on the other person is a good thing. We can easily miss the meaning of what is being said or even miss the key words in conversations if we do not pay full conscious attention. We all have different temperaments and personalities and operate in different ways and on different wave lengths and sometimes it seems as if the two people communicating with one another are speaking two totally different languages.

When couples come to see me for coaching and counselling the most common theme or issue is communication. As couples learn to communicate more consciously with each other they begin to become much more aware of the way in which they contribute or do not contribute to the communication process. They can then both choose to make a few changes to improve it. It really is all about self-awareness and making the choice to take some personal responsibility to change and when this is done, it is amazing how the communication improves.

It is useful to know how we operate and communicate and it is wise to learn how to adjust our communication delivery to match another's when necessary. To connect with people and reflect and communicate back to them effectively we have to learn to listen well. A great way to practice improving our communication and listening skills is to practice answering people with words that connect to what they have said to us.

Where Am 'I' Right Now?

For instance: Peter says *"Are you going straight home after work today?"* You would then reply *"Yes Peter, I am going straight home after work today"*. Or Peter might say, *"I 'felt' that the man in the shop today was ..."* You could reply, *"Yes, I 'felt' that too"*. Rather than *"Yes Peter, I 'saw' that too"*.

This might seem like very basic communication skills to learn, however, give it a try and you may be surprised at how much your listening skills improve in just a few days. Conscious communication is about learning to listen as much as it is about speaking. By communicating in this new way you will set up an energy flow between you and the other person that becomes like a dance. It is a subtle and powerful way to communicate and if you choose to learn it and use it, it will create a nice harmony between you and the people that you communicate with.

Some of the biggest challenges I observe in communication are the reactions and interjections that take place. As you begin to challenge yourself in becoming more conscious about how you communicate with others, try to become even more aware of the way in which you listen, speak and move your body and eyes. For instance, try to see if you can allow other people to complete their sentences before speaking and also be aware of holding the space so that you can complete your sentences without being interrupted by others.

This may take some practice, as does all new boundary work, but once you begin to empower yourself to do so, your communication skills will begin to improve, even if it takes the people around you some time to adjust to your new boundaries and clarity. It often comes as a shock to people when new boundaries and requests are put into place and you can expect to receive a few reactions. This is quite normal. When habits are broken and changed it often takes time for people to accept them. Patience, caution and respect are necessary. Unless we are fully conscious in all of our communications (which generally we are not) there is a tendency for us to speak from a place of reaction rather than from a place of response. If we react or start to blame during a conversation our 'I' presence starts to diminish.

When the blame game or the reaction game begins, it's all over red rover, and any form of conscious communication is lost.

> **You can now probably understand why it is good to have a deeper understanding of how we communicate, operate and act in the world?**

The image of St George and the dragon can be a good reminder of how we can tame the unruly astral aspect of our being. The dragon can be seen as representing the rampant astrality which has to be constantly tamed by our 'I', which is represented by Saint George. The dragon is not slayed but tamed, as our astrality is part of our being and we do not want to destroy this aspect of ourself. We just need to keep this rampant astrality under control – which is not a job for the faint-hearted!

Other myths and legends tell the same story the world over. The story of St Francis of Assisi and the wolf depict a similar image; with the wolf representing the astral aspect of his being.

When we communicate with a lessened 'I' presence we are dimmed in our ability to listen and speak with clarity and full consciousness. Becoming more aware of how we communicate with people is a responsibility we can all learn to take if we wish to build a better, more loving society. Slowing our responses and becoming more aware of what other people are saying to us, beyond their words, is an art which takes time to master. Becoming more aware of another person's movements, facial gestures, tone of voice, breathing patterns and their reactions and responses to us, takes time and practice. The positive feedback from participants at workshops and training programs confirms that these communication exercises and experiences help to improve communication skills, even after just one or two of the basic exercises.

A large part of good communication is about learning to listen.

First old lady *"Isn't it windy!"* Second old lady *"No it's Thursday"* First old lady *"So am I, let's go and have a cup of tea!"*

Some communication exercises can be fun to engage in and are a great way for people to loosen up and learn to communicate in more engaing and conscious ways, without having to think about the process too deeply. The first initial exercises that I use in my personal development workshops and training sessions are generally of a fun nature and designed to get the group energy flowing. It also gives me a good indication of how each person in the group is operating and communicating. Each of us has a certain mode of commuication based on our life experiences, education, family dynamics and position, our awareness and our willingness to learn and grow. By observing this in people through these fun games and exercises I can get a good sense of where they are with their communication skills.

In essence, the art of communication is about giving and receiving and about having a balanced flow of listening and speaking, questions and answers, intellect and creativity, stillness and movement, feelings and emotions, subjectivity and objectivity whilst bringing in the elegant dance of timing and synergy.

As we move more rapidly into the age of electronic social media

The Art of Communication

and electronic communication, much of the art of verbal, personal communication is being lost. More and more people are reverting to and using machines, to communicate with one another. The demise of personal one to one, face to face communication is with us and I sense that it will be increasingly more challenging for the next few generations of people to communicate without the use of electronic gagets. Meanwhile, let us stay focusd on our own speaking and listening skills and our own conscious development in the art of conversation and communication.

As mentioned previously, communication is probably one of, if not the most challenging of all human development work. I love to bring positivity into my communication work and I thoroughly enjoy bringing word exercises and games into my work that empower people.

Chapter Twenty Four

The Three Word Homeopathic Poem

This is a wonderful exercise and is a great way to support people to express themselves and to help them to develop better public speaking skills. This exercise includes potent aspects of both delivering to (giving) and receiving from, a crowd or an audience.

I use this exercise in many aspects of my work to guide people in expressing how they feel about themselves or their life situation. I call the exercise – The Three Word Homeopathic Poem. I call it this because, like the principles of homeopathic medicine, each time the homeopathic remedy is diluted and inverted or shaken, it becomes more potent. As you engage with the exercise you will experience this potency for yourself.

On a piece of paper or in your *Right Now* journal, write down twenty words that describe you in a positive way. Use only positive words. You can use double words, such as 'warm-hearted' if you like, which will count as one word.

For example:

1. Creative

2. Articulate

3. Friendly

4. Artistic

5. Warm hearted

6. Strong

7. Courageous.

And so on to 20

Once you have twenty words written down, wait for a few moments and then look at all of the words.

The next step in the process is to whittle down the words, homoeopathically. You do this by crossing out the words which you connect with the least. At first this may be challenging for you to do. It is not always easy to take away positive words that you have written down to describe yourself. Remember that each time you take a word away it is building up the potency for the next word.

1. Creative

2. ~~Articulate~~

3. Friendly

4. ~~Artistic~~

5. ~~Warm hearted~~

6. ~~Strong~~

7. Courageous

So, go ahead and put a line through four words that you connect with the least and reduce the list from twenty to sixteen words. Take a moment to feel the effect of this and then do it again for four more words that you connect with the least.

Wait for a while and look at the words on your list again.

Take your pen or pencil and cross out four more words. You should now be left with eight words on your list. Take away three more so that you are left with five. And now take away two more words leaving you with three. If you did not manage to write twenty words initially, check the number of words left on your list and cross out enough words so that you are left with just three words. For instance, when you have four words left, delete just one to leave you three.

Once you have your three words, look at them again and write them on the back or the bottom of your paper in the order that feels right for you. Write them down with the words *I am* in front of them.

For example:

"I am Friendly, Courageous and Creative".

Now that you have your three words, you are going to deliver them to the world!

This is a powerful exercise to do with a group of people. See if you can muster up a few people to share this experience with you. If you are reading this alone, pretend that you have a group of good people with you.

The Three Word Homeopathic Poem

If you have not got access to a real stage or cannot construct one, use your imagination and form a stage and conjure up a large audience with several hundred people in it. I get people to image a large auditorium or amphitheatre filled with good people. Now stand up and imagine that you are walking to the back of the stage. Between you and the main stage there is a big red curtain. From behind this curtain, gather your three words in your mind. If this is a bit challenging for you then you can read the words from the paper if you wish to.

Now gather yourself and prepare to step through the chink in the curtain and onto the main stage.

As you step through the curtain, be aware of how you are feeling, physically, emotionally, mentally and spiritually. Take two steps forward and then stand still. Imagine the crowd around you. Imagine them all sitting in a large fully packed amphitheatre. Look around and see them all. Connect to them as if they were really there. Imagine them all looking at you. Feel their presence. Look at them all as slowly and consciously as you can.

Once you have a sense that you have acknowledged the crowd, speak your three words to them in the way that you really want to be heard. Be loud and clear so everyone in the amphitheatre can hear you delivering your words to the world. Example: *"I am Friendly, Courageous and Creative"*.

Once you have said your words, stand very still. Be as still as you can and really allow in and receive the applause from the crowd. Be still for at least half a minute and feel your inner response. Once again, if you do not have a real crowd or audience clapping and cheering you, just imagine it.

Slowly, very slowly, take two steps backwards without turning around, until you reach the curtain. Then step backstage. As you

Where Am 'I' Right Now?

step through the curtain and into the backstage be aware of how you are feeling physically, emotionally, mentally and spiritually. You may feel like shaking, laughing, sighing, shouting, screaming or jumping for joy. When I do this exercise with people I often use a wooden staff as a prop. This gives the participants something to hold and focus on as they do their process.

Variations on this exercise can be made to fit your moods and specific needs. I use this exercise to help people with their facilitation skills and for people who want to confront and work with the more negative aspects of their lives too. It is a great way for people to gauge their balance of giving and receiving and for helping people to find and allow themselves to express more clearly.

I often use this exercise with honouring words in my Men's Groups. We write down twenty words on how we want the world to experience and see us and then we go through the exercise of bringing the twenty words down to three power words. It is always powerful with the men distilling and condensing their twenty words down to three words to capture the essence of who they are and how they want to be seen and understood in the world.

I love to bring a sense of joy and fun and laughter into my work and love it when I am facilitating groups and get to join in and laugh with all the participants. I am never without a fun game or trick up my sleeve and believe that some of the best learning comes through fun and games.

Chapter Twenty Five

Fun and Games

Fifty uuuuppppppp

This is my favourite ball game. The best type of ball to use for this game is one of the light plastic children's play balls about eight inches (twenty centimetres) in diameter. You can play this with two, three, ten or twenty plus people.

So go and find a colleague, some friends or family members and invite them to have some fun. This really is a great game and is a wonderful ice breaker for any group work.

There are only two very simple rules to follow:

Rule number one is – You cannot say sorry!

Rule number two is – You cannot hit the ball twice in a row!

The object of the game is to score over fifty.

I find that if everyone playing Fifty Up calls out the number each time the ball is hit, it makes it more fun and everyone gets involved. First hit – "*One*", second hit – "*Two*", third hit – "*Three*" and so on … I sometimes have to encourage people to speak up and count with the group as some people are challenged to do this.

How the game is played:

One person starts by hitting the ball into the air, and generally within hitting distance to someone else, as the object of the game is to get over fifty hits as a team. The next person hits the ball into the air and then someone else. As long as one person does not hit the ball twice in succession anyone can hit the ball. If someone hits the ball twice in succession, or if the ball hits the floor/ground, then the game starts all over again.

You just keep going and see what score your group can achieve. I have been in groups where we have scored well into the hundreds and even occasionally scoring over two hundred.

If the group is very large, you might like to divide the group into two smaller groups and use two balls.

The Beanbag throwing game/exercise

The bean bag throwing game involves: trust, balance, rhythm, focus, using your senses, giving and receiving and a certain amount of throwing and catching skills.

Small colourful beanbags that are not too loose and which fit nicely into the palms of your hand are good to use. This exercise is performed with two people partnering each other.

How the game is played:

Stand about two or three metres apart from your partner to begin with and gently and slowly throw one of the bean bags to one another for a few minutes to get used to it.

Now introduce the second beanbag and begin to throw them back and forth at the same time, with each person releasing and catching the bean bags at the same time as their partner. It is best to use two hands to catch, placing your hands as close to your chest as you can. You and your partner can move further apart as you improve.

Try and find a connection in your throwing and catching and find a steady rhythm. It is best to throw gently and softly and in a slight arc with an under-arm throw and aim for the chest of the other person each time. Remember that when catching the beanbag, have your hands very close to your chest, then if the bean bag hits your chest it can fall into your hands more easily, especially for the next exciting part of the exercise.

Try and remain focused and keep your feet as still as you can. Find a slow steady rhythm and maintain it. It helps to count out loud together as you are throwing. I find it best to count in a rhythm of three, especially as you progress with the exercise to the next level.

The next level is to catch and throw with your eyes closed.

To begin with, it is easier for only one person to close their eyes and for the other person to keep his or her eyes open to keep the process flowing. As you improve your skills, you can both close your eyes at the same time.

Start by throwing the beanbags to each other in the steady rhythm that you have established. This is where counting helps.

Where Am 'I' Right Now?

Count – one, two, three as you release and catch. As you release the bean bag on the count of three, one of you will close your eyes. If the throwing is accurate, it should reach your chest and hands. The more rhythm and rapport that you have developed with your partner the easier it will be. Once you have your eyes closed, keep them shut for as long as the bean bags keep being thrown and caught. Try to do five, ten or even twenty throws and catches with your eyes closed. You can swap over after a few minutes and the other person can be the one to close their eyes. Once you are used to it you can do the exercise with both people closing their eyes at the same time.

The two games that I have highlighted are a lot of fun and offer opportunities to develop great communication, balance, giving and receiving, as well as catching and throwing skills. I trust that they will bring you lots of fun.

In much of the work that I do I often get a sense that there is a deeper level to it all and that perhaps there is some sort of fate, karma or destiny involved and I love to bring this into the fold in my workshops, specially into the three day Where Am 'I' *Right Now?* personal development workshops. I often end these workshops with a creative process called The Destiny Basket.

The Destiny Basket, and several other games and exercises can be seen on the Where Am 'I' *Right Now?* DVD. See the back of the book for more details

Chapter Twenty Six

The Destiny Basket

The original version of The Destiny Basket was given to me by a friend as a gift for my fortieth birthday. I have further developed it to suit and fit my own work. The version that was given to me really supported me in what I was going through at the time in a very profound way.

I will guide you through the setting up and ritual process that I generally use for a group to give you an idea of how it can be used.

If I am close to home, I generally set up The Destiny Basket using a large copper tub, although any basket, tub or container will suffice. I like to make it a visually enjoyable experience and try to keep everything beautiful by using silks, crystals and even flowers, to adorn the basket and the space.

For a shared group setting, where all the participants are to receive gifts, the number of gifts to go into the basket is always determined by the number of people in each group. Each person in the group is required to bring three gifts, which is planned well in advance, especially if you intend to do this in a workshop setting. I will often give people a couple of weeks to gather their gifts as it becomes part of the whole process that we are engaging in together.

Each person is given instructions to bring three wrapped gifts. The instructions are quite simple – bring three items that you are connected to in some way. Choose items that you are willing to give away but also carry some sort of emotional attachment for you. Examples are: jewellery, toys, books, ornaments, music, photographs, poems, pictures, tools, or precious stones.

In my Destiny Basket experiences, I have received a silver good luck charm, an incense holder, books, CDs, crystals and a small gardening trowel. I have seen people give away and receive a didgeridoo, amazing art works, old personal family items and even a tape measure (which at the time was the perfect gift for the recipient!).

The three gifts from each person are placed in the Destiny Basket and when it is time, the ceremony begins.

This process can take up to two hours if there is a large group. It is important that everyone present has placed their three gifts into the basket. As each person needs to receive three gifts, I often have a few spare gifts kept aside just in case someone forgets!

It is often best that people do not receive one of their own gifts, although I have seen it happen once or twice and it was perfect for the situation at the time. One person begins the process by choosing a gift and they open it.

The process which I use is about connecting the group and connecting the past, present and future. The first gift represents the past. The person who gave the gift tells a short story of what this item represented for them and explains their connection to it; perhaps how they received it themselves and something about the item.

The receiver of the gift then says what they are experiencing from receiving it. They share how they see it as representing something from their own past?

There are a couple of options on how the next steps can proceed:

Option one. A second gift is taken from the basket by the same person who chose the first one. **Option two.** Someone else in the group takes a first gift, followed by everyone else taking their first gift. Depending on which option is chosen, the format or procedure now stays the same throughout the whole process.

The second gift taken from the basket, regardless of the process chosen, represents the present (as in 'now'). The same communication process is followed for the second gift and then a third gift is chosen to represent the future. For all three steps, (past, present and future), the communication process is the same. It starts with the giver and then the receiver. This is done regardless of whether one person is completing all three steps in succession or whether one person goes after the next person in each step. I have worked with both options and each one is equally as effective.

Each gift in the three stages will generally, but not necessarily, have a different giver each time, as the receiver chooses each gift from the basket.

The Destiny Basket ritual is complete when everyone has received their three gifts. Each gift will represent the past, the present and the future for each participant and it is a great way of connecting people. I hope that you enjoy your own Destiny Basket experiences as much as I have enjoyed mine. This is a great thing to do for birthdays and other celebrations and in workshop settings. It does need to be organized well so that it flows smoothly and effectively.

Another variation is for one person to receive all of the gifts in the basket, such as the person having the birthday. This is what happened for me when I received this gift for my fortieth birthday. One gift is taken at a time and each gift is spoken about by the giver and then by the one receiving. It is amazing how the gifts link up, with each one connecting to the next as the stories unfold.

In summary:

For an individual with a celebration you can arrange for everyone to bring their gifts and the individual opens them all. For groups everyone brings three gifts and receives three gifts. This can either be done with the first person opening one present and then moving to the next person or the first person opening three gifts in succession – past, present and future, before the next person does the same.

> **Each now moment in life is a gift; that is why we call it the Present!**

As you unfold your own destiny, see how many gifts you can receive and give away on the journey. Giving and receiving is an art and it takes quite a lot of focus to create a balance.

How are you in giving and receiving? How do you feel about giving? How do you feel about receiving? You can get a good measure and sense of this by remembering the last birthday party or other celebration you had, or attended. Try to remember, what was it like to give someone a present? How did you feel about giving a present? Now remember your own birthday party or celebration. What was it like to receive presents? How did you respond or react to receiving?

I recently offered to help a friend move house and he shared with me his reluctance and difficulty in accepting and receiving my help. He said that giving and helping me move was easy but receiving my help was a real challenge. There are many areas in our lives that require giving and receiving. See if you can get a sense of how and where you can bring this into more balance in your own life.

I know many people who love to give and not receive and many people who love to receive and not give. The secret of course is to find a healthy balance between the two.

When we find a healthy sense of balance between giving and receiving, we become less one-sided, more in harmony with other people and our own sense of equilibrium.

Take some time to see where you are in your life on the giving and receiving scales.

In your journal, write a list of the last ten gifts you gave away and the last ten gifts that you received. Review each one and evaluate for yourself what experiences you had with each one. This will give you an idea of where you are on the scales of giving and receiving.

If you are tilting more towards the comfort zone of giving, work on receiving more. If you are more in the receiving comfort zone, see if you can give more gifts.

One way to bring more balance into our lives is my engaging in a practice of meditation. Giving oneself time and space to meditate and receiving the gifts that meditation can offer and deliver to us can help to bring a wonderful sense of balance.

Chapter Twenty Seven

Meditation and Relaxation

The practice of meditation is thousands of years old and probably as old as humankind itself. It is not difficult to imagine the first humans gazing dreamily up into the heavens or sitting around a fire in a meditative state.

Much has been written and handed down about meditation and there are many schools of thought and different techniques to choose from. I have a simple outlook on meditation to share with people who wish to begin or improve their meditation technique and that is – Find a meditation that suits you! Find a practice that suits your temperament, time management and life style and just do it. If you are new to meditation, I would strongly urge you to be cautious about what you do. I believe that it is a waste of time and effort to choose a meditation technique or practice which is too challenging; where you just end up feeling stressed. In the beginning, I recommend that you find a meditation technique and practice which fits with you and your lifestyle, rather than trying to fit in with it. This way you can ease your way into the world of meditation, knowing that you are more likely to enjoy it and continue with the practice.

While working at the Yarra Valley Living Centre[17] from 1999-2003 and beginning my more serious attempts on meditation, I learnt that I could meditate more easily with some techniques and really

---

17 Also known as the Gawler Foundation, located in the Yarra Valley, Victoria, Australia

struggled with others. I chose to stay with what suited me and slowly challenged myself over the years with more challenging techniques. A lot will depend on whether you are a visual, auditory or kinaesthetic type of person. It will also very much depend on your daily routine and lifestyle. If you are a morning person, morning meditation will be easier for you. If you tend to climb out of bed later in the day, then getting up early in the morning to meditate may be a struggle and you might find that midday or perhaps evening is more suited to you. If you are trying meditation out for the first time or wish to get more comfortable with your meditation practice, try meditating at different times of the day and then choose what feels right for you.

Ian Gawler, the Founder and former Director of the Yarra Valley Living Centre, has created a wide range of meditation books, CDs and DVDs which I highly recommend. A common practice is to find a quiet place, sit in a comfortable position, close your eyes and relax by following your breathing: in-out-in-out.

Thich Nhat Hanh, an insightful Vietnamese Buddhist monk, poet and scholar, offers instructions for a beautiful walking meditation. I find this meditation a wonderful way to connect into the journey of movement and feeling whilst experiencing each careful footstep as it lands on the earth.

At a retreat with one of my special teachers and good friend, Jeff Levin, who established and teaches Life Alignment we learnt a walking and movement meditation based on the Mer-ka-ba.[18]

Steps and hand movements are moved in a specific pattern to broaden one's awareness of space, time and movement. Moving as

---

18 The Mer-ka-ba is an ancient form or symbol that represents both the masculine and feminine principals as one; conjoined to make a whole. Expressed as a solid shape it is seen as a star tetrahedron, a three dimensional, eight pointed star made from two triangular pyramids, one pointing up and the other down.

one in a large group adds another dimension to the meditation, although doing it alone is a powerful experience in itself.

As a didgeridoo player, I love to get into the zone and create a deep place of meditation. Here, in this meditative didgeridoo sound-space, I experience a deep connection to the land, the planet and the universe. One thing that I love to work with in meditation is aligning, balancing and healing the chakras. I do this with the didgeridoo and work with people one to one or in groups of up to twelve people. After people have sat in on one of these powerful experiences they often tell me that they feel much more balanced and connected and in tune with their chakras. I now have an *Aligning and Healing the Chakras with the Didgeridoo and Gongs* DVD for people who cannot get to a live event. (See back of book for more details).

There are many different meditation techniques to choose from. I would suggest that you go and explore some of these techniques for yourself and find which one suits you and work with what feels right for you. I believe that the most important thing with meditation is to just do it!

Setting new goals such as setting the goal to meditate regularly has been a theme throughout this book in both subtle and not so subtle ways. We set goals every day of our lives, whether we are conscious of them or not. I love working with people on creating, setting and achieving goals and spend much time doing this for myself.

Chapter Twenty Eight

Goal Setting

When we set goals we can feel much more empowered, especially if we get to actually achieve them! It is often the choice to enter into a goal setting process in the first place that becomes our ticket to empowerment. Making a choice to do anything positive is empowering and once we get a taste of being empowered it can help to fuel us to follow through and achieve much more in our lives. By stepping into a place of actively trying to achieve our goals we really are stepping into our 'I' presence. It is by stepping in that we begin the process of overcoming some of our basic fears, doubts, inhibitions and self- judgements which can keep us locked into old habits and life patterns that limit or stop us from achieving the things that we wish for and want in our lives. Once our goal has been set we then have a choice of whether we follow through and actively try to achieve our goal or not.

Here is a true goal setting story.

In November 2010, I gave myself a challenge to swim across a large lake close to where I lived. I gave myself until the end of the summer to do it. I was inspired to do this after watching a short movie about a sixty two year old man who walked from Canada to the North Pole – a trek of over 320 kilometres. His name is Raymond Aaron, a motivational speaker and mentor from America. I was inspired by Raymond after meeting him in Australia at a weekend seminar and have been following him for some years to help motivate me to do better in some of my own work.

Where Am 'I' Right Now?

After only three weeks of making the decision, I had swum across the lake and back again – twice!

The first time I did the swim, I was in all sorts of panic as old memories came up of nearly drowning when I was a child. Out in the middle of the lake I had coughing fits and tears in my eyes. I forced myself to go on. I was out further and in deeper water than I had ever been in before and I was terrified. The thought of Raymond walking out in the snow and ice in temperatures of minus forty degrees helped me to keep going.

Finally, reaching the other side of the lake I burst into tears and screamed out with joy and jubilation as I realized that I had broken through some old fears which had kept me locked into a negative and debilitating belief system about drowning.

I have set myself many goals in my life and have not always managed to begin or complete them all, but what I am learning to do now is to try my utmost to follow through with all my goals and dreams, even if it means just taking small steps along the way to achieve them. Writing this book was a big goal for me and hey, it is now in your hands after three years of set-backs, fears and doubts and many other challenges. My first children's book, *Wendy and the Fairy Ring Secret*, took thirteen years from the first ever draft to the final publication. I now have a file filled with manuscripts in various stages of development that will get completed step by step, month by month, week by week, day by day, hour by hour and minute by minute. I even have plans to make a movie!

By following through and attempting to achieve my goals I know I am empowering myself. I know that every time I do this I am loosening and shaking off another fear, another doubt or another aspect which keeps me from standing in my power – in my

'I' presence. See if you can set yourself a few goals so that you too can experience a loosening and shaking off of your fears or doubts about your capabilities.

I recently facilitated a process with several men on goal setting that were keen to push hard and get their goals achieved quickly. It was a wonderful process to work with as we set a range of goals from fairly easy, to moderately challenging, to quite outrageous. In only a couple of weeks we began to realize that the outrageous goals were becoming moderately challenging and the moderately challenging were becoming easy and the easy ones were done in a very short time. One of the men in the group set himself the task of regularly running ten kilometres several times per week. In only a couple of months, he was running fifteen kilometres two or three times a week.

The power of goal setting is remarkable and I highly recommend that you do some today. So, in a short while I will ask you to go and set yourself a small goal to start the process. Set a goal that you know will take some effort to achieve and then set another slightly bigger one and then keep making your goals a bit bigger each time. Doing this in small steps makes the process much easier to achieve and you will be less likely to give up.

I have a goal to sell over one million copies of this book. As I write this I can feel the doubt trying to cling to my shirt tails, trying to creep into my head, but as I focus and hold the vision and know that my goal is set, the doubts begin to fade and disappear. And *Right Now* – who knows, you may be holding the millionth copy!

One sure way to stop doubt is to take action!

Write down your goals and get into action and soon you will be achieving things that you never thought possible.

<u>Where Am 'I' Right Now?</u>

One of the most remarkable books I have read in terms of outlining and achieving personal goals is the book *Think and Grow Rich* by Napoleon Hill. This remarkable book was written over sixty years ago and has sold over seventy millions of copies across the world. If you would like to know where much of the content from *The Secret* came from, this book may give you a few clues.

Whatever your goals are, you will have to set an intention first to start the process of achieving them. If this is new to you or you feel like setting a few bigger goals, then I would suggest seeking some guidance and support so you can actually achieve them. I work with coaches and mentors all the time. I love to be guided and positively challenged by my own coaches as I know that I grow and develop and my business grows and develops with me. Sadly I see many coaches, trainers and teachers going stagnant because they do not set the goal of engaging someone to help them further their own goals and dreams. As my good friend Andrew the Fire Coach says, *"Everyone needs a good coach, even a good coach!"*

Partly due to the release of the highly successful movie and books on *The Secret*, people have been discussing and writing about setting and achieving goals much more openly in the past few years. There has been an upsurge in consciousness around the world and with the release of many new books and movies in this genre it has brought the process of manifestation to the attention to many more people. I would recommend that you seek out and try some of the methods of manifestation being offered and see what works for you. I have personally been reading and studying the work of Esther and Jerry Hicks and Abraham for several years and was delighted to attend a weekend seminar with them in Australia, where I experienced some of their work firsthand.

> **The one thing to learn with all of this visualization, manifestation and goal setting information is that we have to be dedicated, focused, open and ready for miracles.**

In his book, *Think and Grow Rich,* Napoleon Hill gives a very detailed and powerful outline of how to set about and attain our goals. He outlines some key words and aspects of how to set one's mind and attention to achieve what one really wants in life. His main angle is around financial gains. However, his system can be used for any goal, not just financial.

I have also used some of the suggestions, recommendations and tools from *The Secret* and I have had quite a few interesting and successful results. Being a kinaesthetic type person and liking to touch and create, I make manifestation charts with pictures of things I want to have in my life, with the pictures on my charts representing what I would like to manifest into real material items. On one chart that I made, I had a picture of an air balloon and I was gifted a flight in one. I had a picture of a Mitsubishi Delica 4X4 and owned one. I had a picture of a camper van and owned one for a while.

Here is a funny and true story about manifestation to share with you.

I was attending an evening manifestation workshop facilitated by my wife Arleen where we had to visualize and write down a few things that we wanted to manifest. For fun, Arleen suggested that we write down something humorous or something we would not usually write down. Arleen wrote down that she would like to receive a set of hot pink French lacy underwear and I wrote down that I wanted to manifest a diamond.

<u>Where Am 'I' Right Now?</u>

After the workshop I walked to my parked car and as I was about to open the door I noticed something on the road by my feet. I picked it up and was amazed to see in my hand a set of diamonds. Although they shone brightly, they were sadly fake diamonds. It was a set of about twelve tiny fake diamonds set in a silver metal casing that had a magnetic backing. I stuck it to the front of my car and left it there even after selling it a year or so later. It was fun and a big lesson on being clearer about my wishes!

Arleen's wish of receiving a set of hot pink French lacy underwear actualized when we were on a visit to England a few weeks after the workshop. We arrived at my mother's place and she almost immediately produced a brown paper bag and handed it to Arleen. Inside was a set of hot pink French lacy underwear!

The power of visualization and the wish is an untapped field for us to learn more about and use more consciously. Perhaps you would like to explore this for yourself some more.

Write down three things that you wish to happen or you wish to receive and start to visualize them every day and see what happens. It is a good idea to keep things rather simple to begin with. The diamond story that I shared can be a sweet reminder to be clear about your wishes. If you wish to take this further you can do so by downloading the free *Seven Step Goal Setting* e-book from the Conscious Life Development Foundation website.

Goal Setting

I wish you well on your manifestation journey and trust that your wishes will come true. Then again, you may not receive your wishes if you fall prey to one of our greatest enemies when doing goal setting and manifestation work ... and do nothing.

Chapter Twenty Nine

Procrastination

Yes, entertaining our old friend procrastination can be a real downer. I know from my own experience and from conversations with hundreds of people that I have worked with, that even though you may have spent hours, days and perhaps weeks reading this book, you may still not have moved on (very far) from where you were at the very beginning; from the first page.

Even knowing that you have read this book with some interest and have probably taken in some, if not all, of the information, I feel that perhaps you may still not have actually put it into action.

I say this, because, after years of working with people and observing procrastination at work, I know that you may be under its powerful and deliberating spell. The procrastinator in us can be our biggest demon, or, from our new perspective and standpoint, our 'littlest me!'

Having a theory and thinking and feeling good about all that you have read is fine and I am glad that you have managed to reach this point in your awareness and consciousness; however activating your will to put it into action is quite another thing.

So, my question to you is this. Did you do at least four or five of the exercises offered to you in the book? Did you fully engage with at least a few?

Do you remember the dance – 'Think'- tap-tap-tap; 'Feel'- tap-tap-tap; 'Will'- click-click-click. Well, it is now time to click-click-click your will into place.

Ask yourself *Right Now*, have I got the will to follow through with putting this knowledge and information into action? Can I set myself the goal to re-read the book again and follow each exercise thoroughly?

We all have our limitations, excuses, blockages and various degrees of procrastination. These often stop us from moving forward and grasping the moment to really take control of our lives and allow ourselves to become more positive, more aware and more conscious.

So, if you are caught up with procrastination or some other blockage or reaction, can you set yourself the challenge and start the book over again? Can you exert your will and re-read the book again more consciously and make a new real choice to do the exercises?

My deepest wish for you and my final challenge for you is for you to dig deep inside your being and find that will; to connect with your will and challenge yourself to follow through with your thoughts, ideas and feelings while reading this book again and then put it all into powerful action.

<u>Where Am 'I' Right Now?</u>

> **I love the simplicity of the Nike statement –** *"Just Do It!"*

So, with my coaching hat on, I would like to say to you – if you have not suceeeded in doing the exercises and you truly want to make some positive changes in your life, go back to the beginning and start all over again.

I have worn many hats in my life apart from my coaching hat and have been through many challenges, adventures and changes, physically, emotionally, menatlly and spiritually. Read the next chapter to follow some of my story.

Chapter Thirty

Adrian's Story

Early childhood

Born in September 1963 (I was 50 in 2013) I entered the world ready for my journey of being Adrian Dennis Hanks.

My childhood was filled with adventure after adventure. Many hours were spent wandering the countryside tracking and watching animals and birds, and of course, getting up to mischief like most boys love to do. From the age of about six until eleven, I was exposed to several challenging experiences that, in hindsight did set me on my life path of being a coach and counsellor. There are parallels from my childhood that have returned to my life years later, either as a tool for my work or as a reminder of how to do things in a different way that I now acknowledge and embrace. Having done years of Inner Child work to explore and heal some old wounds, especially as part of my counselling and psychotherapy training – many of my old memories, wounds and behaviours are now thankfully tamed and healed.

Mr Gingell, who has now passed over into the spiritual world, was the headmaster at my primary school. He was a very influential figure in my life and I had a lot of respect for him. He had a keen interest in nature, ancient history and energy work, which has been an interest of mine throughout my life. There was a time that I remember fondly when Mr Gingell had all twenty or so children from our class standing around the school grounds in specific positions that he had marked out using dowsing rods. He had each child stand in a place where he said a standing stone would have been standing at some time in the past before the church school was built.

The advice he gave me during my last few days in primary school, before going to the nearby secondary school, is still etched in my memory. *"Be a leader Adrian"*, he said to me, *"Don't be a follower, be a leader"*. Other people have given me similar advice during my life and I have learned to take their words seriously and have chosen to become that leader in many different areas of my life.

The teenage years

Life for me suddenly and dramatically changed in 1977, at the age of fourteen, when the Sex Pistols, Punk Rock, drugs, alcohol, much older girls, sex and politics abruptly arrived in my life. This was not a great mix for a young lad of my age with a growing taste for adventure and risk. During this time, life really was a cocktail of wild adventure and daring. I was introduced to too many things which I was much too young to experience. However, I now realise, that it is because of these experiences that I can now understand and work with youth and adults in a deep and understanding way. Managing to steer, or perhaps dodge my way through and survive these early teenage years without going to hospital or Borstal[19], was remarkable. Several court appearances, a few fines and a stint for twelve weekends at a Youth Attention Centre were the 'rewards' for my unlawful teenage actions. I feel that I got off lightly. Other friends were not so lucky, as several of them ended up in Borstal or prison or dead.

In 1979, when Margaret Thatcher was standing for the position

---

19   Corrective Services for youth

of Prime Minister, we had a 'mock' election at school with several students, including myself, standing as candidates for our preferred parties. At that time in England, there was a comedy program on TV about a revolutionary called Citizen Smith who emanated Che Guevara (Argentinian revolutionary 1928-1967). He (Citizen Smith) was part of a socialist based political organisation called the 'Tooting[20] Popular Front'. As I fancied myself as a young revolutionary, I decided to stand as an independent in the mock school elections with a party called 'The Cirencester Popular Front' (The CPF). I/we polled really well on Election Day, rocking the school establishment with a very high percentage of the vote. The powers that be[21] deemed that voting for me and my party was illegal based on some ridiculous and fictitious grounds – and like the whole of England, the Conservatives won the election. That was a big lesson for me and it has steered my political beliefs and scepticism ever since.

Although bright and inquisitive as a student in both primary and high school, I left school at the age of sixteen without receiving any formal school qualifications. I did not fit the system and was glad to leave. Baking became my career for three years, giving me my first real taste of healthy bread, as one of the bakeries I worked in was part of a health food store. At this time, drinking alcohol and smoking tobacco and marijuana was a big part of my social life. There was also a steady supply of Speed (amphetamines) and LSD. Girlfriends were aplenty and I was very sexually active.

Europe

Early one Monday morning, in late August 1982, whilst at work in the bakery, two good friends asked me if I would like to go overseas

---

20 A suburb of London
21 School teachers and administration

with them. Right there and then, I gave one week's notice to my boss. Eight days later and three days after my nineteenth birthday, I was standing in the streets of Paris ...Voila!

Paris and the surrounding countryside were amazing. We (me and my two friends, Andy and Roger) did several weeks of grape picking in France and Germany. The sense of freedom, new adventure and of course, new foreign girls was exciting. This was the beginning of my love and connection to travelling and for a couple of years I explored Central and Southern Europe with Andy and Roger and a couple of other friends. In 1985, after travelling around Europe together for six months, my girlfriend and I decided to live in West Berlin. Three years of living in Berlin and becoming 'Ein Berliner' was a powerful time for me. My Berlin days led me to a deeper interest in reading, art and writing poetry. Books by Franz Kafka, George Orwell, Hermann Hesse and other great socio-political writers filled my mind with an interest in the wider political world, especially in the politics of Socialism versus Capitalism as I was personally experiencing the political divide between East and West Berlin. Perhaps I would be a politician after all!

Living in West Berlin gave me easy access to Eastern European cities such as Prague, East Berlin, Dresden and Warsaw. In both East and West Berlin I visited many wonderful art galleries, including the Bauhaus Museum and Art Gallery which displayed many works by Kandinsky and Klee, who, during that time were some of my favourite artists.

In 1987, I met the woman who was to become my first wife. She was studying German language at a university in Berlin. She came from Tasmania in Australia and soon after we met, we moved from Berlin to Tasmania. This was quite a culture shock for me – it was like going from a wild psychedelic party to a ballroom dance.

The Berlin wall 'fell' in 1989 and I am so pleased to have had the experience of living in the divided city. As my life includes some of the history of Berlin I often reminisce about this time as being a time of self-discovery and social and political awakening.

Tasmania

After spending the first few months recovering from the culture shock, I settled into the 'Tassie' way of life and spent the next ten years raising four children, scores of chooks, ducks, horses, cows, goats and sheep, while embarking on a new, more organic and healthy life style. During my early years in Tasmania I realized that I was becoming conscious of being on a deeper spiritual life journey. There was a re-awakening of my early childhood spiritual experiences and connections.

My journey of being more self-aware started to unfold and the concept and actuality of living 'in' the moment rather than living 'for' the moment was awakened. At about the age of twenty eight, the habit (addiction) of smoking cigarettes and pot were no longer serving me and needed attending to, along with some other 'bad' habits that I had developed over the years. My life was becoming much richer and more fulfilling with living on our small farm in the country and living a life which had a deeper spiritual meaning felt wonderful.

Baking was my main job for much of the ten years in Tasmania, although many hours were spent working as a biodynamic gardener and farmer on our seven acre property, as well as some time working on the local Steiner school farm. I was learning lots about bio-dynamics – a holistic gardening and farming system which Rudolf Steiner initiated in the early 1920s. Many years of study and practical application, along with the teachings, insights and philosophies of

Anthroposophy, has given me a good foundation for my personal, spiritual and professional work.

During my time in Tasmania, writing and performing poetry, playing the didgeridoo and reconnecting to my childhood love of nature became a big part of my life. Meditation and ongoing spiritual investigation and a deeper interest in human behaviour were becoming part of my everyday life and my future as a personal development coach, counsellor, facilitator and trainer was being hatched. It was, even though I was not fully aware of it at the time, paving the work to come, for my work *Right Now*.

Study and training years

After selling the family property in Tasmania and closing up ten years of life on that beautiful island, we moved to mainland Australia. We moved shortly after the birth of our fourth child. Victoria was all very new to us, but we slowly settled into a new and welcoming community and new way of life. After studying Anthroposophy full time at the Melbourne Rudolf Steiner Teacher Training College in 1998 and gaining Certificate IV in Anthroposophical Studies, my training then began as a Psychophonetics student counsellor and psychotherapist with Yehuda Tagar at Persephone College. During this time of study (1999-2002) I worked at the Yarra Valley Living Centre, more commonly known as the Gawler Foundation, a cancer retreat centre, as the biodynamic gardener and educator. Whilst working there, much time was spent further developing my meditation practice by meditating daily and attending several meditation training workshops with Ian Gawler and other expert meditation teachers.

Working with and amongst so many people dealing with cancer was both a challenging and humbling experience. It gave me a deeper understanding of how to work with people dealing with pain, death, grief and loss. Ian continues to inspire me with his work and I am grateful for the time spent at the Foundation and with him, learning much about being a leader and a pioneer and much about honouring and standing in my own truth and power. After just a couple of months working at The Gawler Foundation, I attended a ten day cancer support program. Many interesting and important things were learnt during this time and on other subsequent programs, where I sat in as a participant or helped to facilitate. One of my fondest memories of working there was a time when I watched a young man, who was seventeen, walk across a suspended, hanging by ropes, log which was being held still by six children/youth, who were dealing with cancer themselves and four support workers, including myself, who were working on a Children with Cancer Program. The sheer determination and grit shown by that young man moved me to tears. He died several months later after arranging his own funeral, even going as far as building his own coffin with his Uncle. After his death I was honoured to receive a small container which held some of his ashes. I scattered them into the wind one quiet morning.

My desert experience – The Black Panther

In November 2001, I went for a week long retreat into The Little Desert, on the Victoria and South Australian borders, 300 kilometres North West of Melbourne. I chose this time as it was the time of my Moon Node – the time when the moon returns to the position it was in at the time of my birth. This was my second moon node. Moon nodes occur every eighteen years, seven months and nine days after our birth. The second moon node arrives at thirty seven years, two months and twenty days after our birth.

Out in the desert, it was hot, dry and very challenging. There were many insights, learning and challenges during that time by myself, but the experience which stands out the most in my memory is the experience with a big Black Panther. Whether this panther was real or imagined, I do not really know, but at the time it was very real for me. This unfolding experience revealed many of my deepest fears and forced me to find and use some deep inner courage to overcome these fears. It taught me to stand in my power and face whatever it was that this Panther represented for me. It was both a terrifying and liberating experience. Being alone and challenging myself during this time of personal transformation, I decided to walk about thirty kilometres into the Little Desert from the small car park where my vehicle was parked. After going through a few personal challenges and emotional outbursts during the first few hours in the hot dry desert, I then saw several large paw prints in the sand, on the shoreline of a beautiful salt lake, which stirred my emotions even more. I told myself they were feline paw prints, which I am certain they were. These paw prints were huge. In my mind they definitely belonged to a big Black Panther. That big Black Panther stalked me for five days!

Walking through sparsely vegetated land, I saw, or imagined I saw, the Panther following me from a distance. After panicking and allowing the fear to override me for a day or so and nearly packing up and leaving, I made a decision to face my fears – to face the Panther. After the second day, every time the Panther appeared, I stopped, sat down, closed my eyes and meditated for a while, consciously forcing myself to keep my eyes closed and trying to steady my breathing and the fear. This was profoundly challenging and also empowering. I am still unsure of the physical reality of this Black Panther. However, about a month later a neighbour knocked on the door of our family home in country Victoria and told me to keep the children indoors as he had just been watching a Black Panther in the bush alongside our house. His story was made even more credible with three or four more sightings that week by people in the local area. Whatever it was that I experienced during my time in the desert, it certainly helped me to overcome many of my old fears[22].

South Africa

My journey with Psychophonetics counselling and psychotherapy continues to be an important part of my life and I use it daily in my vocational, social, spiritual and family life. For me, the three years Psychophonetics training lasted for an extra year, taking place in both Australia and South Africa, due to the principal of the college moving to Cape Town in 2002 and because of my own move to South Africa in 2003.

My marriage was no longer serving me or my wife, and after several months of trying to patch things up, I decided to go overseas for a couple of months to get some perspective. I needed some personal space to make some decisions about what I wanted to do. During that time away a choice was made to leave my marriage of sixteen years. This was a very challenging and confusing time and I often felt very much alone on the journey.

Stepping out and away from my children and heading off alone overseas was one of the most challenging things I think I have ever done and yet, I know, that had I not made this decision, I would not be half the man that I am today. Sometimes tough decisions have to be made – and I know that this was one hell of a tough decision. Even though people had, and perhaps still have their own opinions and judgements on my actions and behaviour, only I know the full story and am the only one who knows the pain, anguish and loneliness that I went through during this time.

---

22 Adrian has written about this experience in a book called *The Black Panther Initiation*.

Where Am 'I' Right Now?

The first stop on my journey overseas was Cape Town, South Africa, to see my good friend and teacher, Yehuda. The plan was to visit for five days, before travelling on to the UK, Europe and finally to Sri Lanka. However, South Africa became my home for almost two years. I never did get to Sri Lanka – but that is a whole other story to be told another day. Even though my second year of study was completed in Australia, I joined the second year class in Cape Town and it changed my life. It was there that I met Arleen. After forming a wonderful deep friendship over a period of eighteen months as Psychophonetics study buddies, where we supported one another through our marriage separations and other issues, we started our more intimate relationship.

At the beginning of 2005, I returned to live in Australia to be near my children again, briefly returning to South Africa for a few weeks later that year to marry Arleen in an amazing two day wedding. We really wanted to begin our marriage in a way which expressed who we really were. Choosing to have a meaningful and open spiritual and shamanic wedding ceremony was a clear statement and an honouring for us both. On the first day, we got married in a beautiful Uniting church in Cape Town, with a few friends and family members present. On the second day, we had an outside sacred ceremony, with over fifty friends and family members, at a sacred site with a local Shaman and Priestess providing a very unique and powerful four hour ceremony.

Looking back at my time in South Africa, it was very much about being alone and redefining who and what I wanted to be. It was a time of personal enquiry and growth. It was my own 'dark night of the soul' – a time of facing myself. There was a knowing deep down in my soul that I had the strength and the courage to go out and get all that I wanted and to be free of my fears and doubts and to be free of other people's opinions, beliefs, concerns or advice. Becoming the master of my own thoughts, feelings, actions and destiny was essential. Choosing to be in a position of making conscious choices and not being trapped by fear, doubt, guilt, rejection, judgment or self-hatred was required. It was a time to face my shadows and come out shining.

Working as a Bio-Dynamic (BD) advisor/consultant on a farm on the outskirts of Johannesburg for twelve months was a wonderful and amazing experience. During this time, under my supervision, the farm was converted from a poorly organised and low producing Organic farm into a healthy and thriving BD farm. I spent about ten days a month on the farm, training and teaching the workers what to do, with several workshops on BD farming delivered and some of the farm workers being trained in the basics of BD farming. During this period I spent time at Botshabelo, an orphanage and village situated about an hour away from the farm. Marion, who runs Botshabelo with her husband Con and their family and other workers, had started the Psychophonetics training in Johannesburg and the first time that we met we had a great connection. Senior third year students, like myself, were invited to do some of our practicum work at Botshabelo, counselling some of the staff and many of the orphaned children. What an amazing and very humbling, and I must say, challenging opportunity and experience it was for me to be there. Working with children who had been sexually and/or physically abused and/or who were affected by HIV/Aids was very emotionally challenging. I feel a deep connection with this special place and that is why a percentage of the sales of this book will go to Botshabelo.

On one particular occasion, we were celebrating up on a hill overlooking the Botshabelo village. I had driven the farm 'bakkie', the South African name for a utility vehicle (Ute), full of workers from the farm to meet the Botshabelo community. I had just finished coordinating about one hundred children and a few adults in a big spiralling procession around the fire when Marion presented me with a Father's Day gift from the Botshabelo children. She knew I was missing my own children and wanted to honour and support me. Tears certainly flowed on that occasion.

I have a very fond memory of one young man on the community. His name is Simon, and at the time he was seventeen and had no legs.

This is my story about Simon.

Simon was a street kid on the streets of Johannesburg. He used to ride the trains with his gang, robbing and stealing as part of his life. One night whilst joy riding on a train, he leapt off, as his mates had done, but did not make it onto the platform. His two legs were severed off right across the top of his thighs, by the train's wheels. He was taken to hospital and woke with the rather insensitive news that he had lost both his legs – he did not know what to do. Somehow he got news of Botshabelo and made contact with them to help him.

Soccer is a big deal in South Africa and the boys and men at Botshabelo love to watch and/or play as often as they can. On the day of my arrival the Botshabelo team were playing in a tournament against several other local teams. It was a big deal as each team had put in several hundred Rand (South African currency) and they all wanted to win the prize pool.

Simon really wanted to go and watch the games but there was no room for him in any of the vehicles, so I told him I would take him in the bakkie. Simon is a big lad, even without his legs and he was very acrobatic. After he had settled into Botshabelo, he joined the in-house karate club and succeeded in getting several belts. Before we ventured off to the soccer matches we went into the local supermarket to get a few snacks and for the sheer fun of it, I put Simon, all eighty plus kilos of him, on my back and piggy-backed him into the shop. The look on people's faces was worth every effort and from then on, Simon and I had lots of fun together.

Simon made a choice to start afresh and he asked Marion if he could start school; something he had never done before. He sat with the little children to begin his education in primary school and slowly but surely settled into a new way of life. He is one inspiring person who is held deeply in my heart. Good on ya Simon!

I see my time in South Africa as a time of personal initiation. It really was a time of facing some of my greatest fears and doubts. It was a time of having to step more fully into my 'I' presence. I left South Africa, after almost two years, stronger, clearer and more in my being than I ever was before. Somewhere deep down I learned to fully accept myself for who and what I am. Coming through this 'initiation' was a big learning process on how to shine my light in the world with a real sense of clarity and worth. I feel Africa is in me and is part of who I am.

A couple of instances which helped to give me this wonderful sense of self and helped to open my heart, were the gifts of a name and a shaman's walking stick. The name was given to me by some of the farm workers on the biodynamic farm. The honour of bestowing the name fell to James, a young black African youth who worked on the farm. They gave me the name Mbandanni (unsure of the correct spelling). They told me it meant – man of honour. The shaman's walking stick was given to me by an old black African lady called Chrissie, who worked for a friend. She named the stick for me as Isi-Dima. Dima means respect. When you return as a man from the bush, after initiation, you now command more respect, and the stick is a sign that you are to be respected.

Where Am 'I' Right Now?

Back to Australia

Now, let me share with you the story of my arrival back in Australia in January 2005 as this will help to give you a clear insight into how to engage with, and use the 'Where Am 'I' *Right Now?*' journaling process.

Arriving back in Australia was a very powerful and empowering time for me. I was without any of my previous material or family possessions, had very little money and was separated from Arleen, my lover and future wife (we were married later that year).

If, I had been asked the question, *"Where are you, Right Now Adrian?"* in January 2005, my answer would have been something like this:

Physically – *"I am living out in nature on a Trade Stock Route; a piece of land just out of town near Armidale NSW. I am sleeping in the back of my $200 unregistered station wagon by night and sleeping and resting in a hammock during the day. I have no money, am in debt and eat only sparingly. On a positive note, I am feeling quite fit and am enjoying the quiet of the bush and finding it refreshing to be washing and swimming in the cool fresh river every morning".*

Emotionally – *"I am in several places. I am engaged to be married to my future wife who is still in South Africa so I am feeling lonely, separate and frustrated. I am also feeling somewhat unworthy to start a new life with someone in the current situation in which I find myself. However, I am feeling in love, loved and supported by my new fiancé and close friends. I am feeling somewhat disconnected from my four children after being away in South Africa and only seeing them for a few times during this time. I am feeling worn out already from having to face starting all over again materialistically with my living arrangements and with my work. I am also feeling the beauty of solitude as I spend time alone in the bush. I would say that my feelings are bitter-sweet right now".*

Mentally – *"I am feeling quite sharp. I have a sense that I am going to be alright no matter what happens, as I know deep within myself that I will pull through this current situation in my life. I am awake to my surroundings and alert to my own personal needs right now. Although I am 'down and out in Armidale', like George Orwell was in 'Down and out in Paris and London', I am mindful of my inner strength and capabilities. Losing the plot is no longer an option".*

Spiritually – *"I am strong. I am meditating regularly and tuning into my spirit guides and keeping my faith. I am living in the realms of nature and I am feeling very connected – even though I am challenged materialistically, I am feeling very strong spiritually".*

I remember driving into Armidale after a few days of living out in the bush and sitting on a park bench in the middle of town and making the decision that I 'would' get somewhere to live and 'would' get some paid work within three days – it happened just two days later!

The journey of building myself up to start my new life in Australia was set in motion from that day and it often acts as a reminder to me of how to stay focused, strong and present. Being 'down and out' was a huge challenge and yet it was one of the most powerful times in my life in terms of personal belief and growth. It gave me a sense of power and the knowledge that I can do anything that I set my mind to do, physically, emotionally, mentally or spiritually.

After spending a solitary and soul searching week in nature, I started working as a counsellor and massage therapist in Armidale, in a small two roomed apartment next to an art gallery. One room housed me and my meagre possessions – a hammock and a few eating utensils and of course my didgeridoo, while the other room became my work space with a massage table, a small table and three chairs borrowed from the woman who owned the art gallery. Soon afterwards, I gained work as a youth worker and a disabilities support worker, which activated many more skills for working with people in different and challenging life situations.

Essentially, since my return to Australia in January 2005, my focus has been on working as a motivational coach, counsellor, facilitator and trainer, creating, developing and facilitating workshops and training programs, as well as devoting time to writing.

Asking myself the question *"Where Am 'I', Right Now?"* while writing this chapter, my response is:

Physically – *"I am feeling fairly fit, swimming regularly in the ocean and in the healing waters of the Ti-tree lake, eating healthy, mostly organic food, not consuming any alcohol (for eight years), doing my morning Yoga, weighing a healthy eighty four kilos and feeling good".*

Emotionally – *"I am able to stand in my being more easily without reacting, judging and projecting (most of the time!). I am currently being challenged with a couple of my children and challenged by some of the global events that are unfolding".*

Mentally – *"I am feeling sharp, aware and am using my mental capacities to write and further develop my work".*

Spiritually – *"I am feeling connected and in touch with my spirit guides and with my own sense of Self and purpose".*

Answering the same four questions again several months later, my response is:

Physically – *"I am feeling fairly fit, weighing a solid eighty four kilos, have started to be more conscious of my diet and am trying* *to stay off gluten as much as I can. I am playing golf again once a fortnight after a break for a few months and I am walking regularly on the beaches and around the lighthouse in Byron Bay".*

Emotionally – *"I am feeling like I am more in my power than previously and am communicating a lot more deeply with Arleen. I have made a deeper connection with several men which has opened up and released some emotional blocks within me".*

Mentally – *"I am feeling sharp, aware and have been using my mental capacities to write and further develop my work. I have started to edit and work on other books".*

Spiritually – *"I am feeling connected and in touch with my spirit guides and with my own sense of Self and purpose. I have started to really focus on daily meditations".*

Reaching fifty and moving on …

Through my forties I knew that by the age of fifty I wanted to be established in my work as an expert in personal, professional and spiritual development. I knew that to honour this, several things would have to unfold; one of which was writing and publishing this book.

The choice and the decision to write this book and to follow through with it has been an amazing experience. I meet many people who dream about writing a book but never pick up a pen or get to type their words onto a computer. I really wanted to write this book and write about the things I have learnt, experienced, been shown and thought about, since consciously working on my own self-development. I guess the choice was made to write and I went ahead and picked up the pen!

Where Am 'I' Right Now?

As a motivational coach, I coach people who wish to be more in touch with their passion and dreams and I love the moment when it all starts to flow for them. Seeing people attain their goals is one of the greatest gifts I receive from this work.

Essentially, my work is all about supporting and positively challenging people on their journey of personal, professional and spiritual development, which I trust I have managed to do for you with what I have written in this book. As I live each year of my life past 50 – all the way up til 106, I want to embrace and work more deeply with my passion of working with people and keep exploring, finding, creating and delivering new, cutting edge and empowering content.

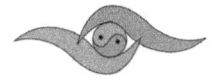

Chapter Thirty One

The Botshabelo Community

The Botshabelo orphanage community is situated about 100 kilometres northwest of Johannesburg in SouthAfrica. It is the home of more than 500 people, including newborn babies, young children, youth and adults. It is a place that I hold deeply in my heart and I love to visit there each year as part of the 'Spirit of Africa Journey', where I lead a group of up to twenty people on a life changing three week journey through South Africa, Namibia, Botswana and Zimbabwe.

Botshabelo was founded by Marion and Con Cloete in 1990 and is dedicated to improving the lives of children who have been orphaned by, or exposed to HIV/AIDS. The community includes an orphanage, school, village, medical clinic, a bakery and an organic farm. Visiting and stepping into the daily life of this community is a very special and eye-opening experience. By getting up close and real with all that is going on, there is no option of not getting emotionally involved. The children are so full of life and inquisitiveness that there is never a dull moment.

Some of my most precious moments have been spent at Botshabelo and I have certainly learned lots about community life, humility, compassion, empathy and gratitude, whilst being there.

To learn more about Botshabelo, and to make a personal donation if you wish to, visit their website.

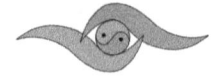

Chapter Thirty Two

Rudolf Steiner

This book would not feel complete if I did not say a few words about Rudolf Steiner. He has been my main spiritual teacher and guide for over twenty years. I have read, studied and worked with many of the initiatives that he brought to the world. He birthed the name Anthroposophy to describe and encapsulate his human-spiritual work. Anthropos meaning Man and Sophia meaning Wisdom: Anthroposophia – Anthroposophy.

I first 'met' Steiner in 1992 when my eldest son began his journey in the Steiner school system, in Tasmania. Soon after this new connection I attended a lecture and workshop on biodynamic agriculture by a bio-dynamic farmer and educator and fast became knee deep in biodynamics and other Anthroposophical initiatives.

After a couple of years of being in the Steiner Community I joined the Anthroposophical Society, becoming a signed up member of the School of Spiritual Science[23] in 1998. Steiner and Anthroposophy are a huge part of my life and after being connected to Steiner for more than twenty years I have come to think of him as a close friend, mentor and guide. Steiner was given a huge spiritual task during his lifetime and I admire him for bringing and doing so much. I see Steiner as a visionary who helped to forge goodness and light into the world, bringing a bright spiritual light in a time

---

23 The School of Spiritual Science consists of several sections, such as an agricultural section, medical, educational, artistic sections and so on. In the General section, regular class meetings are held with a meditative character meant for the development of spiritual capacities.

of great darkness as a guiding beacon for others.

His work has given me more than enough in terms of knowledge, understanding and guidance in my quest for self-mastery. When I read his books and lectures, or engage in something on an experiential level, I know that somewhere, my questions will be answered on a deep level, physically, emotionally, mentally and spiritually.

When I invite the spirit of Steiner into my meditation or into my 'meeting room', where I have discourse with my team of guides, I imagine him being there completely in his 'I' presence. This is one of the great inspirations and visions that I draw upon in times of any self-doubt or imposing fears.

For me, Steiner encompasses the archetype of a human being who has overcome and mastered the self, mastered his shadow-self, or in Anthroposophical terms, mastered his (rampant) astrality and double. It is due to his guidance and influence that I have been able to do much taming of my own shadow astral-self and I am deeply grateful for this connection.

After twenty plus years of studying and working in the field of Anthroposophy and spiritual investigation, I feel that my spiritual 'I' has definitely incarnated. I now look forward to the next steps of the journey and what it has in store for me

I know, from reading many biographical and spiritual books and from working with hundreds of men for the past two decades that the fifties are a time to stand more fully in my power and in my vocational journey.

And on that note, I would like to say thank you for engaging in this journey with me through the book and good luck on your own life journey; wherever it takes you …

Further Information

Services

Coaching – For individuals, couples, groups, businesses and organisations – studio appointments, in-house or by phone or Skype

Counselling and Psychotherapy – For individuals, couples and groups – studio appointments or by phone or Skype

Eco Soul Bush Experience – one and two day outings out in the realms of nature

Facilitation Training (Train the Trainer) – For people who wish to become facilitators or trainers or for people who wish to update and gain new skills

In-house Skills Development – For groups, business and organisations – workshops and training on communication, artistic expression and health and wellbeing

Where am 'I' Right Now? – Workshops, seminars and retreats for personal and spiritual development

Men's Work – Regular local groups and organised events

The Naked Truth – Workshops, seminars and retreats for couples – facilitated by Adrian and Arleen

Didgeridoo – Playing and healing techniques tuition and aligning and healing the chakra with the didgeridoo for individuals, couples and small groups

Spirit of Africa – 21 day spiritual journeys to South Africa, Namibia and Botswana – in August/September each year

Where Am 'I' Right Now?

Recommended reading

The Black Panther Initiation – A book based on a true story by Adrian

Wendy and the Fairy Ring Secret – A wonderful children's book by Adrian

Psychophonetics – holistic counseling and psychotherapy – by Robin Steel (contains chapters by Adrian and Arleen)

Life Alignment – by Philippa Luddock (with a contribution from Arleen)

Think and Grow Rich – by Napoleon Hill

Theosophy – Rudolf Steiner

Speech and Drama – Rudolf Steiner

Knowledge of the Higher Worlds – Rudolf Steiner

Set by the Ancients – Paul and Phoebe Hoogendyk

DVD's

Where Am 'I' Right Now? DVD – A filming of a three day WAIRN? personal development workshop to inspire you and to give you a sense and an experience of what these empowering workshops have to offer you

Eco-Soul Bush Experience DVD – A filming of a one day adventure out in the realms of nature to give you a sense and an experience of what this unique experience can offer you

Didge in 4 Steps DVD – Learn How to Play the Didgeridoo with Adrian – watching this DVD is like being in one of Adrian's live didgeridoo workshops

Aligning and Healing the Chakras with the Didgeridoo and the Gongs DVD – with Adrian and Steve Syms from WowNow Gongs – a two hour film to guide you through your own journey of connecting, aligning and healing your chakras

Angels in the Dust DVD – the story of Botshabelo village orphanage in South Africa

Links

Botshabelo – Community orphanage village in South Africa

www.Botshabelo.org

Arleen Hanks – Life Alignment practitioner and teacher

www.Life-Alignment.com www.AligningLife.org

Psychophonetics – Australia

www.Psychophonetics.com.au

David Styles – Deep Nature Connection

www.DavidStyles.com

Ian Gawler – Meditation and Health and Wellbeing

www.IanGawler.org

Empowering Men – Adrian's Men's work

www.EmpoweringMen.org

Life Alignment – Jeff Levin

www.Life-Alignment.org

Les Peach Didgeridoos – Top quality Australian didgeridoos

www.LesPeach.com

'Conversations' the Game – created by Barry Auchettl

A powerful and inspiring 'game' used to increase and heighten you listening and speaking skills. Fun for anyone from 9-99!

www.ConversationsTheGame.com

Truthology Foundation

Inspiring and educational information on social and political issues and for setting up Foundations

www.Truthology.org.au

Spiritual Events Directory – Sarah Watkins

Marketing, publicity and promotion

www.SpiritualEventsDirectory.com

Pick-a-WooWoo Publishing Group – Julie-Ann Harper

My wonderful publisher

www.pickawoowoo.com

Lightning Source/Ingram Sparks

My book printer and channel distribution

www1.ingramspark.com

Further Information

For more information and for products and services or to contact the author, go to **www.AdrianHanks.com**

As a *Big Thank You* for reading this book I would like to offer you some

Special Bonuses

Free CLDF Membership
Free E-books and Articles
Monthly Global Conscious Awareness Newsletter

Simply go to the website and opt in
www.AdrianHanks.com

Where Am 'I' Right Now?

**Join Adrian and a wonderful group of African guides and facilitators on a twenty one day journey of a life time to South Africa, Namibia, Botswana and Zimbabwe
on the 'Spirit of Africa Journey'**

Every August/September

Visit Sacred Caves, Meet Sangoma's,
Visit Mandela's cell on Robben Island, Boat down the great Zambezi River,
Go on Vehicle and Walking Safaris,
Explore Table Mountain, Visit Victoria Falls,
Visit Botshabelo orphanage
And much, much more …

For more details go to
www.SpiritofAfricaJourney.com

www.ingramcontent.com/pod-product-compliance
Lightning Source LLC
Chambersburg PA
CBHW071906290426
44110CB00013B/1295